ONE GOOD DISH

ONE
GOOD
DISH

david tanis

photographs by gentl & hyers

ARTISAN

NEW YORK

Published by Artisan
A division of Workman Publishing Company, Inc.
225 Varick Street
New York, NY 10014-4381
artisanbooks.com

Published simultaneously in Canada by Thomas Allen & Son, Limited.

Library of Congress Cataloging-in-Publication Data
Tanis, David.
One good dish / David Tanis.
pages cm
Includes index.
ISBN 978-1-57965-467-2
1. One-dish meals. I. Title.
TX840.O53T36 2013
641.82—dc23   2013006289

Design by 50/50

Printed in Singapore

First printing, October 2013

10 9 8 7 6 5 4 3 2 1

Also by David Tanis

A Platter of Figs
Heart of the Artichoke

contents

my kind of dish

The word "dish" has many meanings and can signify a variety of things. It still lingers as a compliment for women ("Some dish!"). Dish is also down-and-dirty gossip. And, when a verbal bully shrinks from our sharp rejoinder, we say, "You can dish it out but you can't take it."

But more often than not, when we hear the word, our thoughts turn to food—and usually to comfort food. A covered dish at a church social. A dish of ice cream. A fine fish dish. Deep-dish pie. Actually, the word "dish" does the same for me: it makes me think of simple, satisfying, casual food.

When I told a friend that my new cookbook was called *One Good Dish,* the response was "So it's about one-dish meals?" Well, yes and no. This book is really an eclectic collection of favorite dishes, some designed to serve one or two, some to feed a table. All are meant to be eaten any time of day, with or without accompaniment. It's a departure from my previous books, which are about "orchestrated" three-course menus. Examining my own eating habits, I realized that while I do enjoy those rustic seasonal multicourse meals, that's not the way I cook and eat day to day. Instead, it's often one good dish and a green salad. Company is welcome.

But there are different ways to gather at the table, and this book reflects that as well. You'll find recipes for snacks, hearty meals, and everything in between. Eggs are featured in many ways; so is good bread. Vegetables play a major role, as do soups. There are meat dishes, too, but in small portions. Some dishes may seem more like tapas than meals, but having several small dishes can be a lovely way to eat. Feel free to combine two or more to make a larger spread—Scorched Sweet Peppers and Onions, Spanish Pork Skewers, and Olive Relish toasts, for example. For a light lunch on a summer day, group Tomato and Egg Salad, Braised Artichoke Antipasto, and Cucumber Spears with Dill. With drinks, serve all three kinds of Salted Nuts along with Mussels on the Half-Shell.

None of these recipes are meant to correspond to a traditional time-of-day-for-a-certain-type-of-food mentality. That is to say, what authority would deny a person a bowl of beans for breakfast or a platter of figs for supper, should that be his or her desire? Midnight is a good time for Spaghetti with Bread Crumbs and Pepper. Tunisian Meatballs are something to make year-round. Rice Porridge with Salted Egg is my kind of comfort food. But then, so is Vegetable Pot-au-feu. For a stellar combination, try pairing Broccoli Rabe Italian-Style with Real Garlic Toast, or serve it as a side dish with steaks or chops.

If it sounds like all these recipes are relatively easy to prepare, they are. And if it seems like the menu is all over the map, it is. The only real requirement for a recipe's inclusion here—wherever it comes from—is for it to be tasty, simple, and real. That's what I mean by one good dish.

There are so many good reasons to stay home and cook. And, even though we may not always have the energy to invest in a complex meal, making one simple, delicious dish (maybe two) is certainly manageable. One good dish, carefully prepared and eaten with pleasure, is an end— and a delight—in itself.

a few good ingredients

Good cooking requires good ingredients, even (or rather, especially) for simple recipes like these. Throughout the book you will see references to good oil, good bread, and so forth. These are the basic elements with which to build a good dish, so they really can't be subpar. It's important not only for flavorful food, but for healthful food as well. Here are some specifics to explain what I mean.

ANCHOVIES: Mediterranean recipes often call for anchovies—either as whole fillets or chopped or mashed—used as seasoning. Although price-friendly grocery store anchovies are fine for melting in warm olive oil, look for high quality anchovies if you want a meatier, sweeter product. Options are salt-packed anchovies from Italy, which require a good rinse as well as deboning; or oil-packed fillets from France or Spain, which are more expensive but worth it.

BREAD: There is nothing better than honest, freshly baked bread, and nothing sadder than a tasteless commercial loaf. Happily, good bread is easier to find these days, better bakeries are popping up, and people generally seem to be more interested in hearth-baked, artisanal breads. When I refer to good bread, it means a French- or Italian-style loaf with structure (instead of an airy interior) and a well-burnished, crisp crust. It may be made from either white or whole wheat flour, and should be comprised of only flour, water, salt, and yeast.

GARLIC: Fresh garlic is really the only choice. Look for firm heads, best found at farmers' markets. The best garlic is new-crop, available in late spring and summer. Stored winter garlic can often be sprouty or blemished, and it needs a bit of trimming. For the best flavor, peel and chop garlic just before using. Day-old chopped raw garlic acquires a strong oxidized taste. (Recipes calling for meats refrigerated overnight in a garlicky marinade, however, are exempt from this rule.)

OLIVES: For black olives, seek out the wrinkly oil-cured ones from Sicily or Morocco, Kalamata from Greece, or Niçoise from the South of France. For green olives, try French Picholine or Lucques, Italian Castelvetrano or Bella di Cerignola, or the small Spanish Arbequina. Canned olives are relatively tasteless, so don't bother.

OLIVE OIL: Olive oil is called for in many of these recipes. When you see "olive oil" in an ingredients list, assume that it is extra virgin, meaning it is from the first "cold" pressing, which makes the best-tasting full-flavored oil. At an Italian grocery or better supermarket, there are many choices labeled extra virgin. Most brands are a blend, perhaps from several producers. These moderately priced oils are appropriate for most kinds of cooking. When a recipe calls for a final drizzle of oil, using a fine single-estate oil (olives picked from only one grove) will greatly enhance the dish. You can buy these in small bottles and reserve them for that special use. Although expensive, they can provide a wonderful fruity or peppery finish. (Don't worry, though: the recipes will still taste fine with a tasty lower-priced oil.)

SALAD GREENS: Rather than use premixed salad greens, which are often less than fresh, make your own salad combination, using small or medium lettuces. Store-bought so-called spring mix usually contains chard, mustard, and beet greens, along with other greens so small and tender they immediately wilt when dressed. Washing lettuce is a pleasant thing to do, and a customized mixture will contain only what you want. Add arugula, watercress, or other greens too, as desired. If you must have convenience, better to buy straight from growers at farmers markets for a melange of somewhat sturdier (and more recently picked) leaves.

SALT: Salt is essential to good cooking. The recipes in this book have all been tested using additive-free kosher salt (even, ironically, the recipes containing pork). Kosher salt has a mild flavor and its larger sized grains are easy to use. Flaky Maldon salt is also mild and pleasant. But there are many other kinds of salt available. Unrefined sea salt has a higher mineral content, which adds both flavor and nutrients, but can taste saltier. It's good for general cooking but may be best appreciated as a final sprinkle or served in a little dish at the table. Avoid refined iodized table salt, which has a harsh taste.

VEGETABLES AND FRUITS: For the best flavor, buy vegetables and fruits in season. Pesticide-free and organic or sustainably grown should always be the first choice. Locally grown produce will always be fresher as well, which means shopping at a farm stand or a store with a commitment to local farmers. If you live in a climate where local produce is limited during much of the year, reach to the back of the pile for the fresh stuff or ask for the most recently shipped. When possible, taste before purchasing.

WATER: Good, pure water makes food taste better. Depending on where you live, municipal tap water may contain elements that alter the flavor of foods prepared with it. Filtered water is recommended for making tea, coffee, or other beverages, and for better-tasting water in general. Charcoal filters, such as the inexpensive pitcher-type filters, remove chlorine and a number of impurities. (To remove chlorine only, fill a large container with tap water and leave uncovered overnight. The chlorine gas will dissipate.)

Fried Bread in the Iberian Manner (page 30)

BREAD MAKES THE MEAL

a loaf's longevity

I'm always on the lookout for excellent bakeries, the kind that produce crisp baguettes and rustic sourdoughs, the good honest loaves. Yet while I enjoy eating bread fresh from the oven, I value, too, the loaf as it ages, on its way to becoming quite another ingredient to inspire a meal. Old bread? You may be surprised how flavorful it can be. At home I always seem to have a cupboard full of aging bread. Day-old bread makes the best toast and crostini, but older (some would say staler) bread can be sliced a bit thinner for another day or two, especially a whole-grain loaf, and still be delicious in its own way. The driest loaves can become croutons for soups, or even the soup itself, like *pappa al pomodoro,* or become a juicy panzanella salad. Did I mention bread crumbs, fine or coarse, and *migas,* fried in olive oil? The point is to use the whole loaf—fresh, day-old, or hard and dry.

Bread baking has always been a passion of mine, and I often make bread at home. Lately I've become enamored of flatbreads, like chapati and pita, which are baked on top of the stove on a hot griddle, hot and ready to devour in minutes. You'll find an example on page 38.

james cagney egg-in-a-hole

As a child, I ate James Cagney eggs at least once a week. I didn't know who James Cagney was, and my mother, who regularly made this dish for breakfast, never told me. Or I never asked. Only much later did I begin to wonder why a slice of bread with a hole punched out and an egg dropped in was named for a movie star who usually played gangsters. The buttered slice was gently fried in a skillet (the little punched-out bread round was fried too). A deft turn of the spatula meant the crisp bread hit the plate with a still-runny yolk inside. Like some other childhood food memories, the dish still haunts me, and I crave it from time to time—even if I do update it by using artisanal bread, a good egg, and olive oil, garlic, hot pepper, and sea salt.   SERVES 1

1 slice good bread

Olive oil or butter

1 good egg

Sea salt and pepper

1 garlic clove, sliced (optional)

Pinch of red pepper flakes

Using a small glass or a cookie cutter, punch a hole in the center of the bread. Lightly paint both sides of the bread with olive oil, as well as the punched-out round (or brush with butter if you prefer).

Heat a cast-iron skillet over medium-high heat. When the pan is hot, lay in the bread. Let it begin to sizzle, then crack the egg into the hole. Season with salt and pepper and sprinkle with the garlic, if using. Brown the little round too, but be careful, as it will cook more quickly. When the bread is golden on one side and the egg is partially set, quickly flip it with a spatula and continue cooking for a minute or two more. A runny yolk is the aim. Sprinkle the top lightly with salt and pepper and a few red pepper flakes.

real garlic toast

Garlic toast, simple as it is, needs precision to be great. Aside from starting with good bread, good olive oil, and fresh garlic, the secret lies in preparing it carefully and eating it immediately. The toast should be neither too pale nor too dark, and it should have a little "give" in the middle. Patience is required. Nurse it along—it can't be rushed over high heat or it will burn. In the end, the effort taken pays off. Plain garlic toast, oil drizzled and sprinkled with sea salt, makes for a simply sublime repast. For a more heightened version, should you happen to be in Italy during the olive harvest in late autumn, visit a *frantoio* to sample the newly pressed oil straight from the mill. There you may be offered garlic toast splashed with luscious green *olio nuovo*, which is ridiculously good. Should you wish to dress up, so to speak, your garlic toast, consider these pairings: a slice of prosciutto or lardo, or a slice of ripe tomato; a smear of ultrafresh ricotta or soft goat cheese, or some strips of roasted pepper; and no one would discourage you from turning your garlic toast into a roast beef sandwich. SERVES 1 OR 2

2 slices good bread,
   cut from a rustic loaf
1 garlic clove

Fruity extra virgin olive oil
Sea salt

Toast the bread using your favorite method; this could be an electric toaster, a broiler, or even a grill set over hot coals. The old-fashioned stovetop *tosta-pane* sold in Italian hardware stores is a great choice as well.

Rub one side of each toast lightly with the garlic clove (for a more garlicky taste, rub aggressively). Drizzle the toasts with some olive oil, then sprinkle with sea salt to taste and serve. If you wish, adorn further according to your own whim.

spaghetti with bread crumbs and pepper

For me, this frugal pasta dish ranks among the best things to eat. It has the same appeal as pasta alla carbonara—and it satisfies even without the pancetta, cheese, and eggs. Crisp, oily bread crumbs seasoned with garlic, pepper, and fennel seeds provide all the flavor. It's good for when you are feeling like a hermit and there is nothing in the cupboard. Once I made a good version of this pasta using a too-small pot and linguine. Hence its then-title, Broken Linguine with Bread Crumbs. It can also be made with smaller shapes like ziti or strozzapretti, and it's especially nice with whole wheat or farro pasta.

SERVES 1

A 4-inch length stale dry baguette or a few slices of dry old French bread

2 tablespoons olive oil, plus more for drizzling

3 to 4 garlic cloves, minced

¼ teaspoon coarsely crushed fennel seeds

Salt and pepper

Red pepper flakes

¼ pound spaghetti, linguine, or other pasta shape

A chunk of Pecorino Romano cheese for grating (optional)

With a serrated knife, saw the baguette, if using, into thin slices. Crumble the bread with your fingers, which will produce a nice mixture of coarse and fine crumbs.

Heat the 2 tablespoons olive oil in a wide skillet over medium heat. Add the crumbs and let them fry gently and slowly take on color, stirring occasionally. When they are golden and crisp, add the garlic and fennel seeds and

cook for a minute or so. Season the crumbs generously with salt and pepper, and add a bold amount of red pepper flakes as well. Remove from the heat.

Cook the pasta in boiling well-salted water until just al dente (usually for less time than the package instructions indicate). Drain and toss with the bread crumb mixture. Drizzle a little more oil. Add grated cheese to taste, if you wish.

niçoise salad on a roll

Although crisp garlic toast is wonderful, sometimes you want the opposite of crisp, as in this Provençal sandwich, called *pan bagnat*. The aim here is to let the juicy interior meld with the bread a bit. It's like a soggy salad (divinely soggy, that is) on a kaiser roll. It can be pared down to contain only tomato, or built up to include roasted peppers, grilled eggplant—even some good canned tuna. Garlic, olive oil, and red wine vinegar are the most important elements. A few anchovies and capers make a nice addition too. Take a basketful to the beach. By the time you get there, your sandwiches will be at their peak.

SERVES 4

1 pound ripe tomatoes, in assorted
   colors if possible

Salt and pepper

2 garlic cloves, minced

2 anchovy fillets, rinsed and roughly
   chopped (optional)

1 teaspoon capers, rinsed

3 tablespoons extra virgin olive oil

2 teaspoons red wine vinegar

Pinch of red pepper flakes

12 basil leaves

4 French rolls or a baguette, split

A few tender parsley leaves

Olive Relish (optional; page 107)

Cut larger tomatoes into thick slices or wedges and smaller ones into halves. Put them in a bowl and season with salt and pepper. Add the garlic, anchovies, if using, capers, olive oil, vinegar, pepper flakes, and half the basil, torn or chopped. Gently toss with the tomatoes and leave for 5 to 10 minutes.

Spoon the tomato salad and its juices onto the bottoms of the rolls (or bottom half of the baguette). Lay the remaining basil leaves and the parsley over the tomatoes. Add a spoonful of olive relish to each roll (or 4 spoonfuls to the baguette), if desired. Replace the top(s) and press lightly. If using a baguette, cut into 4 pieces. Cover the sandwiches with a clean dish towel and wait for an hour or so before serving.

waffle-iron grilled cheese

Who doesn't have touchstone foods from childhood? My aunt Ruth made the best grilled cheese sandwiches, bar none. Decades before most people in this country had ever heard of panini, she used a waffle iron to make them with buttered caraway rye bread and Muenster cheese. This mouthwatering panino was embossed with square dimples, like crisp inverse croutons, encasing cheese that oozed and crisped at the edges. I thought my aunt invented it, but evidently it was a somewhat widespread Midwestern custom. There is no reason not to make it exactly the way she did, but here is the version I prefer these days.   SERVES 1

1 tablespoon butter, softened
2 slices good bread

3 ounces Fontina, Gruyère, or raclette
cheese, sliced or grated
Sea salt (optional)

Heat a waffle iron. Butter the slices of bread. Place 1 slice butter side down on the waffle iron, layer on the cheese, and top with the second bread slice, butter side up. Close the waffle iron and let the sandwich cook for about 2 minutes, until golden brown and crisp on the edges. Sprinkle with salt, if desired.

gorgonzola and walnut crostini

Crostini is the Italian way to say toasts. They differ somewhat from brus-chette, but it's a fine point. Perhaps they are more similar to canapés, yet a bit rustic—they could be cousins. An assortment of several kinds of crostini makes an attractive first course, and they're also great at a party. In Tuscany, chicken liver crostini are famously delicious, as are toasts spread with warm mashed white beans. Paired with a glass of wine, they can be a light meal. These crostini with sweet Gorgonzola, rosemary, caramelized onions, and walnuts are served hot from the oven—a sort of open-faced cheesy Italian rarebit. SERVES 4 TO 6

2 tablespoons olive oil

1 large onion, sliced ¼ inch thick

Salt and pepper

½ teaspoon finely chopped rosemary

Six ¾-inch-thick slices rustic whole-grain bread or ciabatta

3 ounces Gorgonzola dolce

18 to 24 walnut halves

Heat the oil in a wide skillet over medium-high heat. Add the onion and cook, turning frequently, until softened. Season generously with salt and pepper, reduce the heat to medium, and continue cooking for about 5 minutes, until nicely browned. Add the rosemary and transfer to a bowl to cool.

Heat the oven to 400°F, with a rack in the upper third. Put the bread on a baking sheet in one layer. Bake for about 5 minutes, until lightly toasted. Turn over the slices and toast again briefly.

Top each toast with about ½ ounce Gorgonzola, then top with some of the onions and 3 or 4 walnut halves. Bake until bubbling and crisp, 5 to 7 minutes. Cut into wedges if desired.

fried bread
in the iberian manner

In Spain (and in Portugal too), in an effort to waste nothing, old bread is turned into migas, essentially nothing more than rough cubes of dried bread fried in olive oil. A few drops of water, a generous splash of oil, and a goodly amount of garlic seem to magically bring even very dry bread back to life. *Migas*, which originally masqueraded as meat for a poor shepherd's meal, is still prized today as a delicious tapa, served warm and dusted with pimentón. It is undeniably hearty fare, and not a bit fussy. There are, of course, many versions, some made with large bread crumbs instead of cubes. Serve *migas* as a snack with drinks, or as a meal, perhaps with fried eggs.   SERVES 4 TO 6

PHOTOGRAPH ON PAGE 14

A stale 1-pound loaf country bread,
    preferably several days old
Olive oil
2 ounces Spanish chorizo, diced
    (optional)

Salt and pepper
2 garlic cloves, minced
Sweet or hot pimentón

Cut, tear, or break the bread into rough 1-inch chunks. If it is quite dry, moisten with 2 tablespoons cold water and cover with a towel for 30 minutes.

Heat ¼ inch of olive oil in a wide cast-iron skillet over medium heat. Add the bread and let brown gently for 8 to 10 minutes, turning the chunks frequently so they slowly crisp. Push the bread to the side, add the chorizo, if using, and let it sizzle. Toss to distribute and cook for a few minutes. Season the bread with salt and pepper. Add the garlic, stirring well, turn down the heat, and cook for 2 minutes more.

Dust the *migas* lightly with pimentón just before serving.

vietnamese vegetable baguette

Bahn-mi is a wonderful Vietnamese sandwich born of a colonial past. It's built on a French baguette, layered with roast pork, ham, and pâté, but then it suddenly goes Asian with an ample garnish of cucumber, pickled daikon and carrot, cilantro sprigs, and hot pepper. My home version is usually meatless, though, with avocado and egg instead, and plenty spicy. SERVES 4

½ cup julienned peeled carrots

½ cup julienned peeled daikon

½ cup julienned peeled cucumber

Salt

½ teaspoon brown sugar

½ teaspoon fish sauce

½ teaspoon finely chopped serrano
   or fresh Thai chile

½ cup fresh bean sprouts, rinsed

2 tablespoons slivered scallions

6 basil leaves, torn

8 mint leaves, torn

Juice of ½ lime

1 fresh baguette

A few lettuce leaves

A few sprigs cilantro

1 firm ripe avocado, thickly sliced

2 hard-cooked eggs, quartered

Put the julienned carrots, daikon, and cucumber in a medium bowl and season with ½ teaspoon salt and the brown sugar. Add the fish sauce and chile, toss well, and let marinate for 5 minutes.

Add the bean sprouts, scallions, basil, mint, and a squeeze or two of lime juice to the julienned vegetables. Split the baguette lengthwise and line the bottom half with the lettuce leaves and cilantro sprigs. Spoon the vegetables into the loaf. Distribute the avocado and eggs evenly, salt lightly, add the top half of the baguette, and press down gently. Cut into 4 sandwiches.

ham and gruyère bread pudding

A traditional bread-and-butter pudding made with milk, egg, sugar, and spice is for some the ultimate use of an old loaf. Like French toast, it is a frugal way to make a delicious dessert. I usually prefer a savory version with ham and cheese. It's sort of like a quiche, but easier. Adding briefly cooked spinach or chard makes a lovely green version, or sprinkle in a handful of freshly chopped herbs along with the scallions. SERVES 4

4 tablespoons butter, softened

1 day-old French baguette,
    cut into ¼-inch slices

¼ pound good-quality smoked ham,
    diced

6 ounces Gruyère cheese, grated

3 large eggs

2½ cups half-and-half

Salt and pepper

Grated nutmeg

6 scallions, finely slivered

Heat the oven to 375°F. Lightly butter a shallow 2-quart rectangular baking dish. Spread the remaining butter thinly on the slices of baguette. Line the baking dish with half the baguette slices, butter side down. Arrange the ham and half the cheese over the bread. Top with the remaining baguette slices, butter side up, and sprinkle with the remaining cheese.

Beat together the eggs and half-and-half, adding ½ teaspoon salt and pepper to taste. Grate in a little nutmeg, add the scallions, and whisk again. Pour the mixture into the baking dish, pushing down to submerge the bread if necessary.

Bake for about 45 minutes, until the custard is set but still a bit wiggly and the top is nicely browned.

breaded eggplant cutlets

In the poorer regions of Southern Italy, meatless meals are commonplace and eggplant is a favorite stand-in. A properly fried slice of eggplant cloaked in golden bread crumbs can be truly marvelous. Two caveats: first, find fresh, firm eggplants (without seedy centers) and, second, fry the slices gently in plenty of olive oil. For a warm antipasto, top small eggplant cutlets with a bit of fresh mozzarella and basil. For a more substantial dish, serve with a simple, bright tomato sauce. SERVES 4 TO 6

2 pounds small eggplants

Salt and pepper

½ cup all-purpose flour

2 large eggs

1½ cups milk

1 cup coarse homemade bread crumbs,
  fresh or dried

Olive oil

Peel the eggplants and cut into ½-inch slices. Season on both sides with salt and pepper.

Put the flour on a plate. Beat the eggs and milk together in a shallow bowl. Sprinkle a baking sheet generously with about half of the bread crumbs. Dip each slice of eggplant in the flour, then submerge in the egg batter. Remove the eggplant slices from the batter with a slotted spoon and lay them on top of the bread crumbs. Sprinkle heavily with the rest of the bread crumbs, pressing them firmly into the eggplant slices on both sides.

Heat ½ inch of oil in a wide cast-iron skillet over medium-high heat. When the oil is wavy, carefully add some of the breaded eggplant in one layer, without crowding, and fry until golden on the bottom, about 2 minutes. Adjust the heat to keep them from browning too quickly. Turn the slices to cook the other side. Blot on paper towels and cook the remaining eggplant. Serve them plain, sprinkled with salt, or embellished (see headnote).

spicy stovetop flatbreads

Centuries before bread ovens came into use, simple flatbreads were being baked on hot stones. Today there are many kinds of flatbread still being rolled or patted out by hand—chapatis, tortillas, piadine, to name only a few—but now they are baked on an iron griddle.

Freshly milled whole wheat flour and water can make a very good plain dough. To this, I add fenugreek, cilantro, and hot pepper for a flavorful flatbread that is a bit more savory. Serve them hot, dabbed with good butter, thick yogurt, or a fresh creamy cheese.   MAKES 12 BREADS

1½ cups whole wheat flour

½ cup all-purpose flour,
   plus more for dusting

1 teaspoon salt

½ teaspoon turmeric

1 tablespoon dried fenugreek leaves

¼ cup roughly chopped cilantro

1 teaspoon finely chopped green chile

½ cup water, plus more if necessary

4 tablespoons butter or ghee, melted

Put the flours, salt, turmeric, fenugreek, cilantro, and chile into a medium bowl. Add the ½ cup water and the butter and stir with a wooden spoon to gather the dough together. Add a little more water if necessary to make a soft dough. Turn the dough out onto a floured board or countertop and knead for 5 minutes, or until smooth. Cover with plastic wrap and let the dough rest for at least 30 minutes, or up to 4 hours.

Divide the dough into 12 equal pieces and form each piece into a smooth ball. Dust each ball lightly with flour and roll into a flat 6-inch circle.

Heat a well-seasoned cast-iron griddle or skillet over medium-high heat. Carefully place the breads on the hot griddle to cook. Turn after about 2 minutes, so each side is lightly browned and speckled (you may need to adjust the heat throughout cooking to maintain the proper temperature). Brush breads with more butter and sprinkle with salt if desired.

cornmeal popovers

Everybody loves warm corn bread, and these popovers made with fine corn-meal have a similar appeal but are lighter. They're the perfect combination of air and crunch. The batter can be poured into a standard muffin tin for individual popovers or baked in a cast-iron skillet for a big impressive one. (Miniature popovers are good with cocktails.) On a hot summer day, try them for breakfast and wash them down with a glass of cold buttermilk.

MAKES 12 POPOVERS

2 tablespoons butter, softened, for
   greasing the tin

3 large eggs

1 cup milk

⅓ cup buttermilk

⅓ cup water

¾ cup all-purpose flour

¼ cup fine cornmeal

½ teaspoon salt

2 tablespoons butter, melted

Heat the oven to 375°F. Generously butter a standard muffin tin or twelve 4-ounce ramekins. In a bowl, beat the eggs with the milk, buttermilk, and water. Sift together the flour, cornmeal, and salt and stir into the egg mixture to make a thin batter. Add the melted butter and whisk until the batter is smooth. Let stand for at least 30 minutes at room temperature.

To bake, put the buttered muffin tin in the oven for 5 minutes. Then, for each popover, pour ¼ cup batter into each cup of the heated tin. Bake until the popovers are puffed and well browned, 25 to 30 minutes. Serve immediately.

NOTE: If using ramekins, place them on a baking sheet. For a large version, use a shallow 4-cup baking dish.

MY KIND OF SNACK

nibbles for any time of day

You might think this section is all about hors d'oeuvres or tidbits to go with drinks before dinner, and in a way, you would be right. Indeed, any of the following little dishes would be welcome served that way. But I imagine them for the kind of informal, sitting-around-the-table nibbling that happens at other times of day, whenever friends and family gather. After all, a gathering is not a gathering without a little something good to eat.

The verb "to snack," for some reason, has a negative connotation these days. Constant admonitions: No snacking between meals. No "snack food," which is presumably the same as "junk food." But didn't a snack used to be something good? As in, are you hungry?—let me make you a little snack. Or, better have a snack, dinner is hours away. Even the proverbial midnight snack doesn't have to mean something bad. A good snack, for me, should generate a little excitement, and if there's something communal and hands-on about it, so much the better.

a few ways with salted nuts

I recently served these nuts to friends. "Fabulous," they marveled. "Where did you get them?" "I didn't *get* them, I *made* them," I responded. And so can you. My two favorite oven-roasted nuts are Salted Almonds with Rosemary—utterly simple, but they taste meaty, and a bit smoky—and Cashews with Indian Spices—buttery, piquant, and aromatic. Chinese Boiled Peanuts, on the other hand, are not at all crisp or crunchy, but they are quite flavorful from simmering with star anise, chiles, cinnamon, and soy. They make a fine snack with a cold beer and are also delicious sprinkled over steamed rice.

MAKES A SMALL BOWLFUL (ABOUT 1¼ CUPS)

PHOTOGRAPH ON PAGE 42

salted almonds with rosemary

½ pound natural (unblanched) raw almonds

2 or 3 rosemary sprigs

Sea salt

1 tablespoon olive oil

Pinch of pimentón (optional)

Heat the oven to 400°F. Put the almonds in a shallow baking dish, sprinkle with 1 tablespoon water, and toss to moisten. Strip the rosemary leaves from the stems and add them. Add a generous pinch of sea salt and mix with your fingers to combine. Drizzle the almonds with the olive oil, toss once more, and spread in an even layer.

Roast the almonds for 10 to 15 minutes, stirring occasionally for even browning. Take care not to get them too dark—check them frequently, since you don't want them on the verge of burnt. The interior should be golden brown. Sprinkle with a little pimentón, if you wish. Serve warm or at room temperature.

cashews with indian spices

½ teaspoon coriander seeds

½ teaspoon cumin seeds

½ pound natural raw cashews

2 tablespoons melted butter

¼ teaspoon cayenne

¼ teaspoon turmeric

Sea salt

Heat the oven to 400°F. Toast the coriander and cumin seeds in a small dry pan over medium-high heat until fragrant, about 1 minute. Coarsely grind in a spice grinder or with a mortar and pestle.

Spread the cashews in an even layer in a shallow baking dish. Roast for 7 to 10 minutes until barely golden. Drizzle with the melted butter, then sprinkle with the toasted spices, cayenne, and turmeric. Season generously with sea salt and toss to coat. Serve warm or at room temperature.

chinese boiled peanuts

½ pound shelled raw peanuts

¼ cup soy sauce

½ cup packed dark brown sugar

2 or 3 whole star anise

2 or 3 dried red chile peppers

A 1-inch piece of cinnamon stick

Put the peanuts in a small stainless steel or other nonreactive pot, add the soy sauce, sugar, star anise, chile peppers, cinnamon, and 2 cups water, and bring to a boil, then adjust to a gentle simmer. Cook, covered, for 2 hours.

Turn off the heat and let the peanuts cool in their liquid. Drain before serving, but reserve the liquid to store any leftovers (keep refrigerated).

quail eggs with flavored salt

A common British pub snack is an egg boiled and served in its shell with celery salt. Of course, the better the egg, the better the snack. Recently I was served a perfect version at St. John, Fergus Henderson's restaurant in London, where they pounded their own aromatics for the flavored salt.

I like to do something similar with quail eggs, using a salt mixture brightened with cumin and cayenne pepper. Quail eggs are quite beautiful served in their speckled shells, so just have everyone peel his or her own, and pass the salt for dipping. The spicy cumin salt is also delicious sprinkled over raw vegetables or any number of other things. SERVES 4 TO 6

18 quail eggs

2 teaspoons cumin seeds

¼ cup coarse sea salt

Large pinch of cayenne

Bring 4 cups water to a rapid boil in a medium saucepan. Add the quail eggs and cook for 2½ minutes. Immediately cool them in a bowl of ice water for 5 minutes, then drain well and put them in an attractive serving bowl.

Toast the cumin seeds in a dry pan over medium-high heat until fragrant, a minute or so. Coarsely grind the cumin in a spice mill or with a mortar and pestle. Transfer to a small dish, add the salt and cayenne, and stir together.

Pass the eggs and the cumin salt at the table, so each diner can peel and season his or her own.

tomato and egg salad

This luscious juxtaposition of sliced tomatoes and hard-cooked egg with well-seasoned handmade mayonnaise reminds me of two classic old-school dishes. One is a traditional Russian salad, a mixture of cold cooked vegetables lightly bound with mayonnaise and sometimes spooned into halved tomatoes. The other is the French oeuf mayonnaise, the simple bistro standby of hard-cooked egg with mayonnaise and nothing more, except perhaps a lettuce leaf. When well made, both are sensational.

You must have sweet ripe tomatoes and good, fresh farm-raised eggs. And as for the mayonnaise, it's well worth learning how to make, and not nearly the chore you may imagine it to be. Store-bought really doesn't compare and ought not be substituted here.   SERVES 4 TO 6

FOR THE MAYONNAISE

1 large egg yolk

1 tablespoon Dijon mustard

½ cup vegetable oil

Juice of ½ lemon

½ cup olive oil

Salt and pepper

Pinch of cayenne

Red wine vinegar

FOR THE SALAD

4 large eggs

2 pounds small ripe tomatoes

Salt and pepper

1 tablespoon thinly sliced chives

Tarragon or chervil sprigs

To make the mayonnaise, put the egg yolk and mustard in a small bowl and whisk together (see Note). Slowly whisk in the vegetable oil, a teaspoon at a time at first, to form an emulsion, then continue adding oil in a thin stream, whisking constantly, until the mixture has thickened. Whisk in the lemon juice (this will thin the sauce), then carry on whisking in the olive oil. The mayonnaise should have the texture of softly whipped cream; thin with more lemon juice and a few drops of water if necessary. Season with salt and pepper, the cayenne, and a few drops of red wine vinegar.

To make the salad, bring a small pot of water to a rapid boil. Carefully lower the eggs into the water, reduce the heat, and simmer for 8 to 9 minutes. Drain and immediately place in ice water to cool. Drain and peel.

Slice the tomatoes about ½ inch thick and place in one layer on a large platter. Season with salt and pepper. Put a spoonful of mayonnaise on each tomato slice. Top with the eggs, quartered or rough-chopped, and sprinkle with the chives. Garnish with the tarragon sprigs.

NOTE: Although I prefer to whisk the mayonnaise by hand, it's fine to use a handheld mixer, blender, or other device. If you do, you will probably need to thin the sauce with a little more water.

speckled sushi rice with nori

If you want something light and tasty to offer your guests with drinks or tea, try this colorful vegetarian sushi rice salad. It is seasoned with a rice vinegar dressing, then sprinkled with sesame seeds, shiso, and cucumber. Everyone simply wraps a spoonful of the rice in a small piece of nori, for a casual hands-on snack. It is not difficult to make respectable sushi rice at home. Just make sure not to overcook it—you want firm grains, so be sure to cool the rice as soon as it is done. SERVES 4 TO 6

2 cups sushi rice

A 2-inch square of dried kombu, rinsed

3 tablespoons rice vinegar

2 tablespoons sugar

1 teaspoon salt

1 tablespoon mirin

$\frac{1}{2}$ pound seedless cucumber, peeled and cut into thin half-moons

2 tablespoons snipped shiso leaves

1 tablespoon Fresh-Pickled Ginger (page 98), finely chopped

2 teaspoons toasted sesame seeds

6 scallions, thinly slivered

Toasted nori sheets

Wash the rice well and drain. Bring 2$\frac{1}{2}$ cups water to a boil in a small pot, add the rice and kombu, and let simmer for 1 minute. Put on the lid, turn the heat to low, and cook for 15 minutes. Remove the rice from the heat and let rest, covered, for 5 minutes. Transfer the rice to a baking sheet and spread it out so that it cools quickly to room temperature.

While the rice is cooking, combine the rice vinegar, sugar, salt, and mirin in a small saucepan, bring to a simmer, and simmer for 1 minute. Let cool.

Put the rice in a wide shallow bowl. Pour the seasoned vinegar over and fluff gently with two wooden spoons. Garnish with the cucumber, and sprinkle with the shiso, pickled ginger, sesame seeds, and scallions. Serve with the toasted nori sheets for making simple hand rolls.

cheese in a jar

Throughout the Mediterranean, cheesemakers have traditionally preserved their fresh cheeses in jars of olive oil, often with the addition of wild herb branches. It is a glorious snack to make at home. After only a few days in a flavorful marinade, it's ready to eat with a good crusty loaf or with Real Garlic Toast (page 18). Make sure to get a little herby oil in each bite. Cheese in a jar is handy to take on a picnic too—and just as nice for an indoor picnic at the kitchen table. SERVES 4 TO 6

½ pound fresh goat cheese log or mild
  feta

A few thyme branches

A few rosemary sprigs

A bay leaf

2 garlic cloves, halved

A few black peppercorns

About 1 cup olive oil

Slice the cheese into 2-inch chunks. Carefully layer the cheese in a clean jar or glass bowl, adding the thyme branches, rosemary sprigs, bay leaf, garlic, and peppercorns as you go. Pour over enough olive oil to cover. Seal tightly and refrigerate for at least several days before serving. This keeps, refrigerated, for up to 1 month.

Feta cheese (left) and goat cheese (right)

cucumber spears with dill

I discovered the method for these salady spears quite accidentally one day when I was preparing traditional fermented dill pickles. I happened to nibble on a cucumber spear only an hour after the seasoning went on. To my surprise, it already tasted really good in its not-quite-pickled state. Now if I want something pickle-like in a hurry, I make these. It's simple: just cucumbers, garlic, salt, red pepper flakes, vinegar (sometimes a bit of lime juice too), and herbs.

These cucumbers are crisp and neither too salty nor too acidic. Good for a snack, or on a relish plate, they're really a step up from "crudités." Make a batch, eat them an hour later or the next day.   **SERVES 4 TO 6**

1½ pounds small cucumbers,
  such as kirbys or Persians
Salt and pepper
3 garlic cloves, very thinly sliced
½ teaspoon red pepper flakes

½ teaspoon thyme leaves
2 tablespoons white wine vinegar
1 tablespoon chopped dill, tarragon,
  or parsley
Juice of 1 lime

Peel the cucumbers and cut them into spears. Put them in a porcelain, glass, or stainless steel bowl and season generously with salt and pepper. Add the garlic, red pepper flakes, thyme, and vinegar and toss well. Let marinate for at least an hour, chilled.

Just before serving, add the chopped dill and lime juice and toss.

moroccan carrots

A common Moroccan salad is made with cooked and coarsely mashed carrots. I first learned about it reading Paula Wolfert's cookbooks, then sampled it during my own travels to North Africa. Sparked with lemon and fragrant with toasted spices, it's an easy dish to love. Look for preserved lemons at Middle Eastern groceries or make your own.   SERVES 4 TO 6

2 pounds carrots, peeled

Salt and pepper

½ teaspoon cumin seeds

½ teaspoon coriander seeds

3 tablespoons lemon juice

½ teaspoon garlic, smashed to a paste
   with a little salt

1 teaspoon grated ginger

Large pinch of cayenne

¼ cup olive oil

2 to 3 ounces feta cheese or
   ricotta salata, crumbled

A handful of olives

1 small preserved lemon, rinsed,
   pulp removed and discarded,
   rind diced (optional)

2 tablespoons chopped cilantro

1 tablespoon thinly sliced scallion

Put the carrots in a pot of well-salted water, bring to a simmer, and cook until tender, about 15 minutes. Drain and cool to room temperature.

Toast the cumin and coriander seeds in a small dry pan over medium-high heat until fragrant, about 1 minute. Coarsely grind the seeds in a spice mill or with a mortar and pestle.

To make the vinaigrette, put the lemon juice in a small bowl, and season with salt and pepper. Add the cumin and coriander seeds, garlic, ginger, and cayenne. Whisk in the olive oil.

Put the carrots in a bowl and, using a potato masher, crush them a bit, leaving them fairly chunky. Dress with the vinaigrette and transfer to a serving platter. Garnish with the crumbled cheese and olives. Sprinkle with the preserved lemon, if using, the cilantro, and scallion.

cold chinese chicken

I love cold chicken: cold roast chicken, cold fried chicken, perhaps especially cold boiled chicken. It is a most welcome snack on a hot day.

This is an easy dish, put together in minutes and abandoned for an hour over a low flame. Try to cook it a day ahead and let its flavors deepen with a night in the fridge. To serve, sprinkle the ice-cold jellied chicken with sesame oil and scallions, then give it a squeeze of lime. If you want something extra, add cucumber, avocado, and crisp lettuce leaves. Or take off the skin, shred the chicken, and have it with cold noodles.

Buy the best chicken you can, even if it costs more (it will). Factory chickens always taste flabby, no matter what you do. Choose a free-range bird for the flavor, the food politics, and, not least, the meaty thighs. SERVES 4 TO 6

6 large bone-in chicken thighs
  (about 2 pounds)
Salt and pepper
A 2-inch piece of ginger, peeled and
  thickly sliced
4 garlic cloves, sliced
3 star anise

4 scallions, 2 trimmed and left whole,
  2 slivered
3 tablespoons chopped cilantro
1 jalapeño, thinly sliced (optional)
2 tablespoons toasted sesame oil
Lime wedges

Season the chicken thighs generously with salt and pepper. Put them in a pot and barely cover with cold water. Add the ginger, garlic, star anise, and the 2 whole scallions, bring to a gentle boil, and skim any rising foam. Turn the heat to very low, cover, and cook at a bare simmer for 1 hour.

Transfer the thighs to a bowl to cool. Skim the fat from the surface of the cooking liquid. Over high heat, reduce the liquid by half, about 10 minutes.

CONTINUED

Strain the broth over the thighs, let cool, then cover and refrigerate for at least several hours, or overnight.

To serve, arrange the chicken on a platter, leaving some of the jellied broth clinging to it. Lightly sprinkle with salt and pepper. Top with the slivered scallions, cilantro, and, if you like, jalapeño slices. Drizzle with the sesame oil and surround with lime wedges to serve.

radishes à la crème

Only four ingredients—radishes, salt, pepper, and crème fraîche—yet they make an extremely tasty raw vegetable first course. If you can, make it with the wonderfully sharp black radishes, still relatively scarce in the States but available at some farmers' markets. Or use a combination of red radishes, daikon, or pink-and-green-striped watermelon radishes. You can even use tender young turnips. The only work is in the slicing. A mandoline is the best tool to ensure the slices are uniformly thin.   SERVES 4

½ pound large red radishes or daikon

Sea salt

¼ cup crème fraîche, or a little more

A few drops of milk (optional)

Pepper

With a mandoline or a sharp knife, slice the radishes as thin as possible. Arrange the slices on a platter. Sprinkle lightly with salt.

If the crème fraîche is quite thick, beat it with a spoon for a minute to lighten it up, or thin with a few drops of milk or water. Spoon it generously over the sliced radishes. Finish with as much freshly ground pepper as you like.

OPTIONAL EMBELLISHMENTS

A drizzle of fruity olive oil, about 1 tablespoon, is a delicious indulgence spooned over the crème fraîche at the last minute. Or garnish with spicy radish sprouts and chopped chives. You can also serve the radish salad on thinly sliced rye bread for great little open-faced sandwiches.

potato salad
with peppers and olives

Even though there are a thousand and one ways to make a good potato salad, generally speaking, I prefer the kind with oil and vinegar, served at room temperature or slightly warm.

When peppers are in season, roast them for this colorful Mediterranean potato salad. Potatoes marry well with the salty olives and anchovies, and strips of sweet pepper add balance.   SERVES 4 TO 6

Salt and pepper

2 pounds medium potatoes,
   such as Yukon Gold or
   German Butterball

A bay leaf

1 large thyme branch

1 small shallot, finely diced

2 garlic cloves, smashed to a paste with
   a little salt

¼ cup red wine vinegar

1 teaspoon Dijon mustard

4 anchovy fillets, rinsed and chopped

⅓ cup olive oil

2 red bell peppers, roasted (see Note),
   peeled, seeded, and cut into ½-inch-
   wide strips

A handful of black olives

A few basil leaves

Bring a large pot of well-salted water to a boil. Add the potatoes, bay leaf, and thyme branch and cook at a brisk simmer until the potatoes are easily pierced with a skewer but still firm, about 30 minutes. Drain and let cool slightly.

While the potatoes are cooking, make the vinaigrette: Put the shallot and garlic in a small bowl and add the red wine vinegar and a pinch of salt. Add the mustard and anchovies, then whisk in the olive oil.

Peel the potatoes and carefully cut into ¼-inch slices. Put the potatoes and peppers in a wide salad bowl and season with salt and pepper. Pour over

the vinaigrette and gently toss, using your fingers to coat the vegetables well. Garnish with the black olives and basil leaves.

NOTE: To roast peppers, place them directly over the flames of a gas stovetop burner, over hot coals on a grill, or under the broiler as close to the heat as possible. Turn them frequently, using tongs, until the skins are completely blistered and blackened. Put them on a plate to cool. (I don't recommend covering them to steam or rinsing them with water, although many cooks do.)

To peel, cut the peppers in half lengthwise and remove the seeds. The skins come off easily by scraping gently with a knife.

polenta "pizza" with crumbled sage

This is one of those serendipitous, stumbled-upon creations. I had made a big pot of polenta, and I poured the leftovers into a baking dish in a thin layer. The next day, foraging in the fridge for lunch, I came upon the polenta, a little fresh mozzarella, a little Parmesan (or was it Pecorino?). To make a pizza of sorts, I layered on the cheeses, added a splash of oil, crumbled over a handful of dried sage leaves, and put it into a hot oven. The result was completely satisfying. So what if it's not truly a pizza?—though perhaps it has a culinary ancestor somewhere, since there's really nothing new under the sun. SERVES 4

Salt

1 cup stone-ground polenta

½ pound fresh mozzarella

½ cup grated Parmigiano-Reggiano or
   Pecorino Romano cheese

Extra virgin olive oil for drizzling

Leaves from 1 bunch dried fresh sage
   (see Note)

Red pepper flakes

Pepper

Bring 4 cups water to a boil in a large heavy saucepan and add 2 teaspoons salt. Whisk in the polenta and continue whisking as it begins to bubble. After a minute or two, when the polenta has thickened a bit, reduce the heat to low and let cook gently, stirring occasionally, for about 45 minutes, until thickened and smooth, with no raw cornmeal taste. If the polenta gets too thick as it cooks, add a bit more water. Remove a spoonful and cool, then taste and adjust the seasoning, if necessary.

Spread the polenta on a lightly oiled baking dish to a thickness of ½ inch. Let cool and set, preferably overnight, in the refrigerator.

Heat the oven to 400°F, with a rack in the top third. Tear the mozzarella into big shreds and scatter over the polenta. Top with the Parmesan. Drizzle lightly with oil and crumble the sage leaves on top.

Bake the polenta until the cheese is bubbling and lightly browned, 10 to 15 minutes. Sprinkle with red pepper flakes and freshly ground black pepper to taste and let cool slightly.

Serve cut into rough wedges or squares.

NOTE: You can dry a bunch of fresh sage by leaving it on a windowsill for a day or two. Freshly dried sage is quite flavorful, but if you don't get around to this, don't substitute sage from a jar—use a little chopped rosemary instead.

mussels on the half-shell

While a bowl of steamed mussels can make a great simple feast for one or two, here is a different way to think about mussels, more like tapas. Served on a large platter, their black shells glistening, they go fast at a cocktail gathering. I like to make them two ways: a hot version, baked with herbs and garlicky bread crumbs, and a cold version, topped with a robust vinaigrette. Both are delicious, and both can be mostly prepared in advance. SERVES 4 TO 6

hot mussels on the half-shell

2 pounds mussels

2 tablespoons olive oil

½ cup coarse bread crumbs

2 garlic cloves, minced

2 tablespoons chopped parsley

1 teaspoon chopped thyme

Pinch of cayenne

Salt and pepper

Lemon wedges

Heat the oven to 400°F, with a rack in the upper third. Scrub and debeard the mussels.

Heat 1 tablespoon of the olive oil in a wide deep skillet over high heat. Add the mussels, cover, and let steam open, 3 to 4 minutes. Let cool, then remove and discard the top shells, leaving the mussels attached to their remaining half-shells. Place the mussels on a baking sheet.

In a small bowl, stir together the bread crumbs, garlic, parsley, thyme, and cayenne. Season with salt and pepper and stir in the remaining 1 tablespoon olive oil. Top each mussel with a generous spoonful of the mixture.

Bake until the crumbs are golden, about 10 minutes. Serve the mussels with lemon wedges and eat them straightaway.

cold mussels on the half-shell

2½ pounds mussels

1 tablespoon olive oil

FOR THE VINAIGRETTE

1 large shallot, finely diced

2 tablespoons red wine vinegar

Salt and pepper

1 teaspoon Dijon mustard

3 tablepoons olive oil

1 tablespoon capers, rinsed and
roughly chopped

2 tablespoons chopped parsley

1 tablespoon slivered chives or
scallions

2 teaspoons chopped tarragon or
thyme

Lemon wedges

Scrub and debeard the mussels.

Heat the olive oil in a wide deep skillet over high heat. Add the mussels, cover, and let steam open, 3 to 4 minutes. Let cool, then remove and discard the top shells, leaving the mussels attached to their remaining half-shells. Place on a serving platter.

To make the vinaigrette, put the shallot in a small bowl. Add the red wine vinegar and a good pinch each of salt and pepper. Stir in the mustard to dissolve. Whisk in the olive oil, then stir in the capers, parsley, chives, and tarragon. Taste and adjust the seasoning.

Spoon a little vinaigrette over each mussel and serve immediately, with lemon wedges.

From left: Cold Mussels on the Half-Shell; Hot Mussels on the Half-Shell

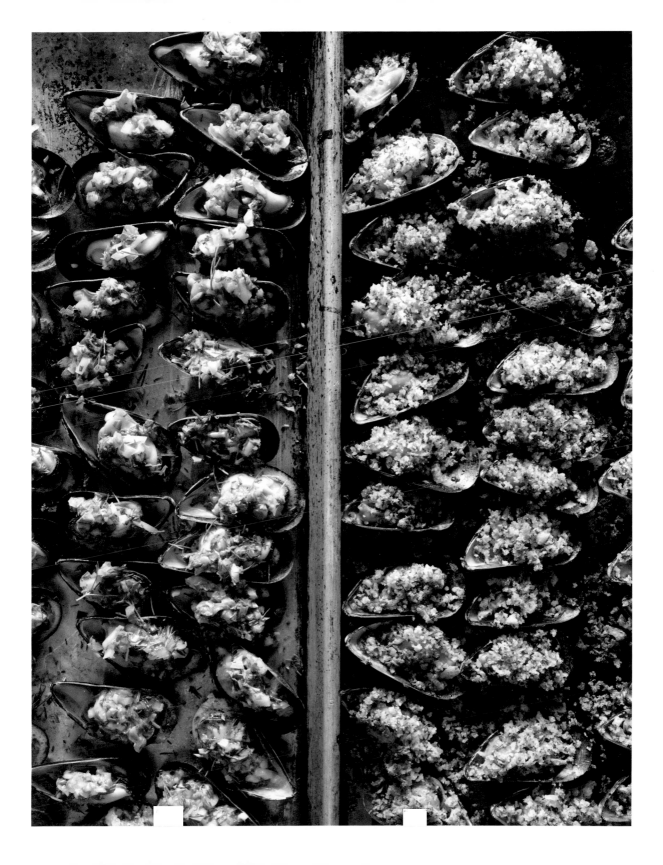

prosciutto and fruit

Because so many mediocre versions of prosciutto and melon are served in restaurants, many people may consider the pairing trite, passé, or just uninteresting. In fact, when the melon is perfectly ripe and the prosciutto is good, their classic salty-and-sweet combination can be heavenly. For that matter, there is a lot to be said for eating prosciutto with fruit throughout the year, using whatever fruit happens to be at its peak: apricot, cherry, melon, nectarine, peach, grape, fig, pear, apple, persimmon. Serve the sweetest fruit you can get.

In season, pears and prosciutto make perfect partners. The best ripe pears will be firm with unblemished skins and will yield to gentle pressure at the "neck."

For a casual stand-up snack, have everyone wrap a piece of fruit with a little bit of sliced prosciutto. Or, if you prefer something more formal, compose individual plates and serve with knives and forks. In either case, consider adding a complementary herb, like basil, parsley, spicy cress, or hyssop. I suggest tearing the prosciutto slices into long, wide ribbons. It's more natural looking and easier to arrange. SERVES 4 TO 6

2 ripe Comice or Anjou pears, or
    similar quantity other seasonal fruit

4 to 6 slices best-quality prosciutto
    (approximately 2 ounces)
A few arugula leaves

Just before serving, quarter, peel, and core the pears. (If the pears are large, halve each quarter.) Put them on a platter. Tear the prosciutto slices into wide ribbons and drape loosely over and around the pears, then scatter the arugula over the top.

red beet salad

Beets can be roasted, boiled, steamed, or turned into chips, but try them raw for this grated beet salad. You can shred them on the large holes of a box grater or cut them into fine julienne—either way, prepare for the likelihood of beet juice splashed everywhere. The grated bloodred vegetable vaguely resembles chopped beef at first glance, so I decided to season this dish like steak tartare, with mustard, shallot, capers, and cornichons. The beet flavor, however, is unmistakably sweet and undeniably vegetarian. Eat it for lunch, with hard-cooked eggs and watercress, or try it with smoked salmon.

SERVES 4 TO 6

1 pound beets, peeled

Salt and pepper

1 large shallot, finely diced

2 tablespoons red wine vinegar

2 teaspoons Dijon mustard

1 teaspoon finely chopped jalapeño or
   a generous pinch of cayenne

1 tablespoon capers, rinsed and
   roughly chopped

¼ cup olive oil

3 tablespoons chopped parsley

3 tablespoons thinly sliced scallions

12 cornichons

2 hard-cooked eggs, quartered or
   chopped (optional)

With a food processor or box grater, julienne or grate the beets (or cut them by hand). Put in a bowl, season with salt and pepper, and toss well.

Put the shallot in a small bowl and add the red wine vinegar and a good pinch of salt. Stir in the mustard, jalapeño, and capers, then whisk in the olive oil to make a thick dressing. Add the chopped parsley and scallions.

Dress the beets with the mixture and let marinate for 10 minutes. Transfer to a serving platter. Garnish with the cornichons. Add hard-cooked eggs, if desired.

mackerel rillettes

In the old days in France, rillettes (essentially very tasty pâté-like potted meat) were always made from pork, duck, or goose, well-seasoned and rather fatty. Spread on a freshly baked baguette, they are still a fine thing. Now rillettes are concocted from almost anything imaginable, and why not? Fishy versions are frequently composed of salmon or shellfish mixed with butter. (However, a tuna salad sandwich I had on a recent Air France flight was called rillettes de thon, and this seemed a rather too glorified name.) I still dream about the mackerel rillettes served by a feisty young Parisian chef. She poached fresh mackerel in a flavorful white wine broth. At home, I use smoked mackerel fillets (or sometimes canned sardines). MAKES ABOUT 1 CUP; SERVES 6

½ pound (2 sticks) unsalted butter, softened

½ pound smoked mackerel fillets, skin removed

½ teaspoon grated lemon zest

1 tablespoon lemon juice

Pinch of cayenne

Pinch of ground allspice

Salt and pepper

1 tablespoon thinly sliced chives

1 tablespoon chopped parsley or chervil

½ teaspoon finely chopped thyme

Baguette slices or dark rye bread

Put the softened butter in a bowl. With your fingers, break the mackerel into medium flakes and add to the bowl. Add the lemon zest, lemon juice, cayenne, and allspice and mix well with a wooden spoon or spatula, mashing the fish into the butter. Season with salt and pepper, then stir in the chives, parsley, and thyme. Refrigerate for several hours, or overnight; bring to room temperature before serving.

Spread the rillettes on baguette slices or on dense, dark rye bread.

braised artichoke antipasto

This antipasto is a homemade, and better, version of the sort you find in jars at an Italian deli. If you can get baby artichokes, they are lovely braised this way, but medium artichokes work well too. (Zucchini or eggplant are also options.) They're simmered in a fair amount of olive oil with aromatics, tomato, white wine, and a touch of vinegar. Delicious warm, they are even better served at room temperature. SERVES 4

1 lemon, halved

2 pounds baby artichokes

1/2 cup olive oil

1 medium onion, cut into small dice

1 small fennel bulb, trimmed and cut into small dice

1 large carrot, peeled and cut into small dice

Salt and pepper

3 garlic cloves, minced

1 tablespoon tomato paste

Large pinch of red pepper flakes

1 cup diced peeled tomato

2 tablespoons red wine vinegar

1/2 cup white wine

1 teaspoon finely chopped fresh marjoram or 1/2 teaspoon dried oregano

2 tablespoons chopped parsley

1 tablespoon chopped mint

Squeeze the lemon juice into a bowl of cold water. Peel the tough outer leaves from each artichoke, then trim the top and stem end of each artichoke and halve lengthwise. Place in the acidulated water to keep them from darkening. (If using medium artichokes, remove the tough outer leaves, cut 1 inch off the top of each, and trim the stem end. Halve lengthwise and remove the central hairy choke with a soupspoon. Cut into quarters or sixths and place in the acidulated water.)

CONTINUED

In a wide stainless steel skillet, heat the olive oil over medium heat. Add the onion, fennel, and carrot, season with salt and pepper, and cook gently until softened, about 5 minutes. Stir in the garlic and tomato paste and raise the heat to medium-high. Add the red pepper flakes, diced tomato, and vinegar, stir to combine, and cook for 1 minute. Add the drained artichokes and the wine, season once more with salt, and put on the lid. Reduce the heat to a low simmer, cover, and cook for about 15 minutes, until the artichokes are tender.

Add the marjoram, mix the artichokes and vegetables gently, and transfer to a shallow serving bowl. Let marinate for several hours or refrigerate overnight, then bring to room temperature. Just before serving, sprinkle with the freshly chopped parsley and mint.

seaweed salad
with sesame dressing

It's always nice when the food you crave is actually good for you. Seaweed, sometimes called sea vegetable (perhaps to make it sound less like a weed), is a delicious, highly nutritious, edible marine algae. You can check Japanese groceries for more exotic kinds of salt-packed seaweeds, but many supermarkets and health food stores sell user-friendly packages of dried seaweed. This recipe uses two commonly available types, reddish-purple dulse and bright green wakame. Both simply need bathing in cold water for a few minutes to soften and ready them for use. The salad is tossed with a dressing of sesame oil, ginger, and soy. I like it with grilled or steamed fish, or simply served with sliced cucumber and avocado. SERVES 4

1 ounce dried red dulse seaweed

1 ounce dried green wakame seaweed

FOR THE DRESSING

2 tablespoons rice vinegar

2 teaspoons sugar

2 teaspoons grated ginger

½ teaspoon wasabi powder

2 teaspoons soy sauce

1 tablespoon toasted sesame oil

Juice of 1 lime

Sea salt

1 small carrot, peeled and sliced paper-thin

4 red radishes, thinly sliced

A 2-ounce piece of daikon, peeled and thinly sliced

1 small cucumber, peeled and thinly sliced

1 firm but ripe avocado, halved, pitted, peeled, and sliced

1 teaspoon toasted white sesame seeds

1 teaspoon toasted black sesame seeds

2 teaspoons toasted hulled pumpkin seeds (pepitas)

4 scallions, slivered

CONTINUED

Put the dulse and wakame in a large bowl and cover with cold water. Let soak for 5 to 10 minutes, until softened. Drain and pat dry. Cut into rough 2-inch pieces. Arrange on a platter.

To make the dressing, whisk together the rice vinegar, sugar, ginger, wasabi powder, soy sauce, and sesame oil in a small bowl.

Spoon half the dressing over the seaweed, add the lime juice, and toss gently. Taste and add a small amount of salt if necessary. Surround the salad with the carrot, radishes, daikon, cucumber, and avocado. Season lightly with salt and drizzle with the remaining dressing. Sprinkle the salad with the white and black sesame seeds, pumpkin seeds, and scallions.

North African Red Sauce (page 91) and Middle Eastern Green Sauce (page 90)

A DAB OF THIS AND THAT

superior homemade condiments

In the beginning, of course, pickles, chutneys, salsas, relishes, even salad dressings were always made at home. Now we have somehow come to believe that everyday condiments are impossible to make and must be purchased in jars. While there may be some good brands, and buying ready-made is convenient, a look at the label usually reveals unpronounceable ingredients, along with thickeners, sweeteners, and "natural flavors," a term that is always a little unnerving. So it makes sense that they're absolutely better when you make them yourself. Stirring them up is easy, and quite a pleasurable activity.

If you don't want to depend on some manufacturer's idea of flavor, here is a small collection of condiments you can easily produce at home. Some, like Tomato-Onion Chutney, are best made in advance; others, like Anchovy-Garlic Spread, can be prepared quickly at the last minute.

middle eastern green sauce

This traditional hot green, herby condiment is served in little jars at my favorite falafel joint in Paris (they serve jars of harissa too)—when they're in the mood to make it. I always ask for it, but some days it's simply not there. No point in asking why, all you get is a shrug. A day without green sauce is a sad one, so I came up with my own, which, slathered into a pita with hummus and tomatoes (or a little grilled lamb), tastes mighty authentic. Try it too in non–Middle Eastern ways, on fried eggs and hash browns, or to brighten a Yankee pot roast. MAKES ¾ CUP

PHOTOGRAPH ON PAGE 88

1 teaspoon cumin seeds

1 teaspoon coriander seeds

Leaves from 1 small bunch parsley

Leaves and tender stems from 1 small
  bunch cilantro

2 serrano or jalapeño chiles

3 garlic cloves

6 scallions

½ teaspoon salt

¼ cup olive oil

Toast the cumin and coriander seeds in a small dry pan over medium-high heat until fragrant, about 1 minute. Coarsely grind in a spice mill or with a mortar and pestle.

Coarsely chop the parsley, cilantro, chiles, garlic, and scallions. Pulse with the salt in a food processor or blender until you have a rough puree.

Transfer the herb puree to a bowl and stir in the ground spices and olive oil. This is best the day it is made.

north african red sauce

All over North Africa, this hot red pepper sauce, known as harissa, is in demand. You can buy it in tubes or cans, but homemade harissa is superior.

Harissa is very useful in the kitchen. Burgers of every kind are improved immeasurably with just a dab. Stir a little into the broth when you're cooking chickpeas or braising chicken, or into thick bean soups. Or use a spoonful in vegetable salads or to give oomph to a vinaigrette. New Mexico or guajillo chiles are a good choice for dried red peppers and have a reliable heat level.

MAKES ¾ CUP

PHOTOGRAPH ON PAGE 88

10 to 12 large dried chile peppers, such as New Mexico or guajillo (about 3 ounces)

1 teaspoon cumin seeds

1 teaspoon coriander seeds

1 teaspoon caraway seeds

3 garlic cloves, minced

½ teaspoon salt

¼ cup olive oil, plus a little more

Remove the stems and seeds from the chiles. Put the chiles in a small pot, cover with water, and bring to a boil, then reduce the heat to a simmer and cook for about 15 minutes, until the chiles have softened. Drain, reserving 1 cup of the soaking water. Let the chiles cool.

Toast the cumin, coriander, and caraway seeds in a small dry pan over medium-high heat until fragrant, about 1 minute. Coarsely grind in a spice mill or with a mortar and pestle.

In a food processor or blender, combine the chiles, garlic, salt, and olive oil and blend at high speed, adding a little of the reserved soaking water if necessary to form a smooth paste. Add the spices and blend for 1 minute more.

Transfer the sauce to a jar and drizzle a bit of olive oil over the top. It will keep for a month in the refrigerator.

anchovy-garlic spread

Start with the best anchovy fillets you can find, imported salted ones or a jar of high-quality oil-packed. Then quickly combine with just a few other ingredients to make an oily, garlicky spread that's good for all sorts of things. I like it on warm toasted bread with drinks. Added to a bit of softened butter with chopped parsley, it's a great sauce for steaks, chops, or grilled fish. With a squeeze of lemon juice, it can be a dip for raw vegetables. Or add a spoonful to salad dressings or simple pastas. Even those who claim to dislike anchovies are usually converted. MAKES ¼ CUP

4 salt-packed anchovies or 8 oil-
   packed anchovy fillets
Lukewarm milk (optional)
2 garlic cloves
Salt and pepper

¼ cup olive oil
½ teaspoon grated lemon zest
Pinch of red pepper flakes or cayenne
   (optional)

If using salt-packed anchovies, soak them in cold water to soften for 5 minutes. Peel the fillets away from the bones with your fingers and rub off any bits of scale or fin. Rinse the fillets and blot dry with paper towels. If using oil-packed fillets, rinse briefly in the milk and blot dry.

Pound the garlic to a paste with a little salt in a mortar (or just use a knife to chop the ingredients together). Add the anchovy fillets and pound to a rough paste. Stir in the olive oil, black pepper to taste, and lemon zest. Add the red pepper flakes, if you like.

italian hot pepper oil

In sit-down pizzerias all over Italy, there are always two condiments on the table. One is a bottle of fruity extra virgin olive oil. The other is a small wine bottle with a pour spout, filled with *olio santo,* hot-red-pepper-infused olive oil. Diners choose whether to anoint their individual pizzas with one, the other, or both. This spicy oil is good for drizzling on lots of things besides pizza—bean soups, crostini of all kinds, and steamed or boiled greens or vegetables, to name just a few.   MAKES 1 CUP

1 cup olive oil

2 tablespoons red pepper flakes

1 teaspoon crushed fennel seeds

1 small rosemary sprig

In a small stainless steel saucepan, heat the oil over medium-high heat to 120°F (use an instant-read thermometer). Turn off the heat and add the red pepper flakes and fennel seeds. Let steep until cool. Strain if desired.

Pour the oil into a clean jar, add the rosemary sprig, and store at cool room temperature.

VARIATION: asian hot oil

1 cup peanut or safflower oil

12 small dried red chile peppers

1 teaspoon Sichuan peppercorns

1 teaspoon cayenne

1 tablespoon toasted sesame oil

In a small stainless steel saucepan, heat the oil over medium-high heat to 120°F (use an instant-read thermometer). Turn off the heat and add the chiles, peppercorns, cayenne, and sesame oil. Let steep until cool. Strain if desired.

Pour the oil into a clean jar and store at cool room temperature.

tomato-onion chutney

Long-simmered chutneys are a bit of a project, but it's lovely to have a jar or two in the pantry, especially this one made with ripe, red tomatoes. Chutney needn't accompany only authentic Indian dishes. A spoonful can also complement a good roast chicken or a leg of lamb, even a plate of scrambled eggs at midnight.   MAKES 4 CUPS

2 tablespoons vegetable oil

1 teaspoon mustard seeds

1 teaspoon nigella seeds

1/2 teaspoon cumin seeds

1/2 teaspoon fennel seeds

2 cups finely diced onions

6 garlic cloves, thinly sliced

2 teaspoons salt

8 small dried red chile peppers

4 cups chopped ripe tomatoes

1/2 cup white wine vinegar

A 2-inch chunk of ginger, peeled and
    cut into fine slivers

2 cups raw sugar or packed dark
    brown sugar

1 cup golden raisins

1/4 teaspoon cayenne

Heat the oil in a heavy stainless steel or enameled pot over medium heat. Add the mustard, nigella, cumin, and fennel seeds and let them fry gently until fragrant, about 2 minutes. Add the onions and garlic, sprinkle with the salt, and cook, stirring occasionally, until softened, about 10 minutes.

Add the hot peppers, tomatoes, vinegar, ginger, and sugar, turn the heat to medium-high, and mash the tomatoes and sugar together with a wooden spoon. Bring to a boil, then reduce the heat to a simmer and cook, stirring frequently, until the chutney has thickened nicely, about 45 minutes.

Add the raisins and cayenne (more if you like it extra spicy) and cook for 10 minutes. Taste and adjust the seasoning. Ladle into clean jars. The chutney will keep for 1 month, refrigerated, or up to 6 months in the freezer. If you process it for canning, it will keep for a year.

fresh-pickled ginger

Pickled ginger is delicious, and it's easy to make at home, without artificial color or MSG. All you need is a knob of aromatic fresh ginger plus a little salt, sugar, and rice vinegar. You can add a slice of red beet to give it a hint of pink, or leave it its natural golden color. This makes a small batch, and it takes only an hour or so for the pickle to be ready. Any you don't use will keep for a couple of weeks in the refrigerator. MAKES ¼ CUP

1 tablespoon sugar

1 teaspoon salt

3 tablespoons rice vinegar

A 3-inch piece of ginger, peeled and sliced as thin as possible (see Note)

1 slice of red beet (optional, for color)

Combine the sugar, salt, and vinegar in a small jar and stir to dissolve the sugar and salt. Add the ginger and beet, if using. Make sure the ginger is completely submerged. Leave at room temperature for at least an hour, or up to several hours, before serving. Refrigerate any leftovers.

NOTE: Use a mandoline or a sharp thin knife to cut the ginger into nearly paper-thin slices. Make slices along the grain, not across it.

quick scallion kimchee

Although the classic long-fermented cabbage-based kimchee is fairly easy to make, it does take time. This version with scallions is ridiculously simple and ready in a day or two. I learned how to make it from my friend Russell, a Los Angeles–born cook whose Korean mother made it throughout his childhood. Russell serves it to accompany perfectly steamed rice and simple grilled fish, a lovely combination. I like it chopped and stirred into a bowl of brothy ramen-style noodles, or tucked into a ham sandwich. MAKES 2 CUPS

4 bunches scallions

2 teaspoons salt

4 garlic cloves, thinly sliced

1 tablespoon raw sugar or
   dark brown sugar

1 tablespoon grated ginger

¼ cup Korean red pepper flakes

1 tablespoon toasted sesame oil

1 tablespoon toasted sesame seeds

1 tablespoon fish sauce

1 tablespoon rice vinegar

Trim the scallions and cut into 3-inch lengths. Put them in a glass or ceramic bowl, sprinkle with the salt, and let stand for 10 minutes.

Mix together the garlic, sugar, ginger, red pepper flakes, sesame oil, sesame seeds, fish sauce, and rice vinegar. Add to the scallions and toss well to coat.

Lay a plate over the bowl and leave in a warm place (at least 70°F) for 24 hours. Or, for a stronger-tasting kimchee, let ripen for up to 72 hours. It will keep for a month, refrigerated.

mrs. paganelli's "pesto"

For years I worked with Carl, an Italian-American raised in a San Francisco suburb. He wasn't a professionally trained cook, but having grown up in a traditional multigenerational Italian family, he'd learned a lot from his relatives, most of whom were great cooks. He was always describing the feasts his clan organized, and I always gleaned a cooking tip from him. One day I saw him chopping up basil and garlic with a knife, then stirring in a generous amount of olive oil. He used it to flavor some stewed zucchini. "This is what my mother called pesto," he said, but it wasn't at all like the thick green pesto I knew. I marveled at how quickly the basil flavored the oil; it's rather ingenious. Drizzle it over most any vegetable, or stir into a pasta dish.

MAKES ABOUT 1 CUP

1 cup basil leaves

4 garlic cloves, finely chopped

¾ cup extra virgin olive oil

Salt and pepper

With a sharp knife, slice the basil into ¼-inch-wide strips, then roughly chop. Put the basil in a small bowl, add the garlic, and stir in the olive oil. Season with salt and pepper. Leave the pesto at room temperature for 15 minutes to let the flavors infuse. This is best used the same day.

mustard from scratch

It's fun (and easy) to make mustard at home. In bygone days, it was considered a normal kitchen task. After all, the simplest mustard is just a mixture of ground mustard seeds, vinegar, and salt.

My friend Charles concocts his quickly, from that mustard powder sold in a yellow tin to accompany grilled lamb chops (a long-standing tradition in his family). Following his example, I was inspired to experiment with mustard making in my own kitchen. This is a slightly grainy mustard, and rather hot and spicy. MAKES ABOUT ½ CUP

3 tablespoons black or brown mustard
    seeds
3 tablespoons dry mustard powder

1 tablespoon white wine vinegar
½ teaspoon salt
¼ cup cold water

Coarsely grind the mustard seeds in a spice mill; open the lid carefully—the mustard oil released in grinding may make your eyes tear. (If you have a deep heavy mortar, you can grind the seeds in that.) Put the ground mustard in a small glass or ceramic bowl. Add the mustard powder, vinegar, and salt, then add the cold water, stirring well. Leave to ripen for at least 30 minutes before using. Store in the refrigerator for up to 2 weeks.

VARIATION: **mustard cream**

This mustard sauce is good with raw, smoked, or grilled fish or with cold chicken or sliced avocados.   MAKES ½ CUP

½ cup crème fraîche or lightly
   whipped heavy cream (about ⅓ cup
   before whipping)
1 tablespoon Mustard from Scratch
   (recipe above)

Pinch of cayenne
Pinch of sugar
2 teaspoons grated horseradish
½ teaspoon grated lemon zest
Salt and pepper

Put the crème fraîche in a bowl and stir in the mustard, cayenne, sugar, horseradish, and lemon zest. Season to taste with salt and pepper. Chill for 30 minutes to let the flavors infuse.

olive relish, black or green

The Provençal olive relish called *tapenade* is deep-flavored and earthy. My French friends would never think of making their own, because they have so many good artisanal versions available to them, but here it's wiser to make it at home. Tapenade is perfect picnic food, easily transported. Just add bread, cheese, and a bottle of wine. It's also a great condiment with grilled or roasted chicken, lamb, or fish, or as a spread in a sandwich. For a quick snack or antipasto, drizzle a spoonful of tapenade, thinned with a little oil, over slices of fresh mozzarella or on hard-cooked eggs.   MAKES ¾ CUP

black olive relish

Use pitted Niçoise, Kalamata, or wrinkly oil-cured olives, or a combination. If making a coarse-chopped version, consider adding minced red onion and chopped fresh marjoram.

1 cup pitted black olives (see headnote)

2 garlic cloves, minced

4 anchovy fillets, rinsed and roughly chopped (optional)

2 teaspoons capers, rinsed

½ teaspoon red pepper flakes (optional)

1 tablespoon red wine vinegar

¼ cup olive oil

Salt and pepper

Put the olives, garlic, anchovies (if using), and capers in a food processor and pulse for a minute or two, until you have a rough paste (or process longer for a smoother paste). Add the red pepper flakes (if using), red wine vinegar, and olive oil and pulse to combine. Season to taste with salt and pepper.

green olive relish

Lemon and thyme add brightness, and parsley and scallions reinforce the "greenness." Use briny green olives, such as French Picholine or Italian Bella di Cerignola.

1 cup pitted green olives

2 garlic cloves, minced

4 anchovy fillets, rinsed and roughly chopped (optional)

2 teaspoons capers, rinsed

½ teaspoon grated lemon zest

1 teaspoon chopped thyme

¼ cup olive oil

2 tablespoons chopped parsley

1 tablespoon slivered scallion

Pinch of cayenne

Salt and pepper

Put the olives, garlic, anchovies (if using), and capers in a food processor and pulse for a minute or two, until you have a rough paste (or process longer for a smoother paste). Add the lemon zest, thyme, and olive oil and pulse to combine. Transfer to a bowl.

Stir in the parsley, scallion, and cayenne. Season to taste with salt and pepper.

From top: Black Olive Relish and Green Olive Relish

Very Green Fish Stew (page 138)

EATING WITH A SPOON

pleasure in a bowl

There is something comforting and elemental about a spoon. It's not as aggressive as a knife and fork. In fact, as infants, we all began eating real meals at the receiving end of a spoon. There's also a kind of primal comfort in wrapping your hands around a warm bowl; making a meal of a bowl of soup can be deeply satisfying. When you think of foods from around the world, many of the most enjoyable are the bowl and spoon type: Asian dumplings in broth, the bean soups of Italy, Indian dals. Whatever their character, thick or thin, good soups are always pleasing and sustaining.

Soup can also feel somewhat cleansing, if one has become a bit overindulgent in the food and drink department. After such a spell, I may opt for a few days of what I have come to refer to as the Soup and Wine Diet. The rules are fairly simple: eat as much soup as you like, and still have a little wine with dinner.

In this chapter, in addition to soups, there are other somewhat "soupy" dishes. You'll find examples such as Spanish Garbanzo Bean Stew, Clams in the Shell with Fennel and Parsley, and Tunisian Meatballs that also beg to be eaten with a spoon.

save-your-life garlic soup

This strictly bare-cupboard Provençal soup is insanely good. The ingredients are nothing more than a lot of garlic, some sage leaves, water, a little olive oil, salt, and pepper. It takes only 10 to 15 minutes to cook, but when you taste it, you'll swear it is long-simmered chicken broth.

Like chicken broth, garlic soup is said to have all sorts of medicinal properties. It apparently can both prevent and cure hangovers, and even aid digestion. It also makes a perfect light lunch or supper on a hot summer day when you don't much feel like cooking. Many versions—including this one— add a poached egg, which makes it more of a meal. And some cooks whisk a beaten egg into the broth to make it creamy.   SERVES 4

2 heads garlic, preferably new-crop, separated into cloves (about 16 medium cloves) and peeled

2 tablespoons extra virgin olive oil

12 sage leaves

Salt and pepper

6 cups water

4 eggs

4 slices bread, lightly toasted

Chopped parsley, scallions, or chives

Slice or roughly chop the garlic cloves. Warm the oil in a heavy pot over medium heat. Add the garlic and sage and let sizzle a bit without browning, about 2 minutes. Season with about 1 teaspoon salt and a few grinds of pepper. Add the water and bring to a boil over high heat, then lower to a brisk simmer. Cook for 10 to 15 minutes. Taste and adjust seasoning.

Ladle about an inch of the soup into a skillet and bring to a brisk simmer over medium heat. Carefully crack the eggs into the pan and poach for about 3 minutes.

To serve, place a slice of toast in each soup bowl and top with a poached egg. Ladle the soup over the eggs and sprinkle with a little parsley.

confetti vegetable broth

This simple little soup is beautiful and delicious. The main trick is to cut the ingredients into ultratiny dice—confetti, if you will. That way, the vegetables cook quite rapidly and contribute their flavor to the soup, making essentially a sort of quick, very fresh-tasting vegetable stock. If you do happen to have a little homemade chicken stock on hand, use it instead of water, but it's not necessary. I often make just enough for my own lunch, and it really only takes a handful of chopped vegetables. I begin with a finely diced onion and ad-lib from there, depending on the season. SERVES 1 OR 2

1½ teaspoons olive oil or butter

A 1-cup mixture of finely diced
   vegetables, such as onion, leek,
   carrot, fennel, and zucchini

Salt and pepper

1 garlic clove, minced (optional)

2 cups water

Chopped basil, parsley, or scallions

Squeeze of lime or lemon juice or a few
   drops of vinegar (optional)

Heat the oil in a small pot over medium heat until sizzling gently. Add the vegetables and cook for 2 minutes. Season well with salt and pepper and add the garlic, if using. Add the water, bring to a simmer, and simmer until the vegetables are just tender, about 5 minutes.

Add the chopped basil and a squeeze of citrus juice, if you wish.

spanish garbanzo bean stew

When I first tasted this wonderful, earthy soup, called *potaje* in Spanish, all I wanted was more. Chunky and substantial, it is a homely dish made from garbanzo beans, potatoes, and a little pork. The recipe below feeds a few, but you could make a big potful for a larger gathering. Like other stews, the flavor improves if made a day ahead. Serve with red wine, radishes, and coarse crusty bread. Flamenco music too, if possible.   SERVES 4 TO 6

1 cup dried garbanzo beans, soaked
   overnight in cold water and drained

¾ pound pork belly (or 1 pig's foot,
   about 1½ pounds)

1 medium carrot

1 small onion, stuck with 1 clove

1 bay leaf

10 cups water

Salt and pepper

2 tablespoons olive oil

2 large onions, diced

6 garlic cloves, minced

½ pound Spanish chorizo, diced

2 teaspoons pimentón

2 pounds Yukon Gold potatoes, peeled
   and cut into 1-inch chunks

Put the garbanzos in a large pot, add the pork belly (or pig's foot), carrot, clove-stuck onion, bay leaf, water, and 1 tablespoon of salt. Bring to a boil, skim off the foam, and simmer for about 1 hour, until the garbanzos are tender. Turn off the heat. Drain, reserving the liquid.

Heat the oil in a heavy soup pot over medium-high heat. Add the diced onions and cook until softened, about 5 minutes. Add the garlic and chorizo and stir to coat. Season well with salt and pepper and add the pimentón. Add the garbanzos and 8 cups of the cooking liquid, bring just to a simmer, and cook gently for 45 minutes. Add the potatoes and continue cooking until the potatoes are quite tender, about 15 minutes. Taste and adjust the seasoning.

Remove the pork belly, slice thickly (or remove the meat from the pig's foot and chop it), and return it to the pot. Ladle the soup into bowls.

egyptian breakfast beans

I have always liked eating beans for breakfast, whether it's pinto beans cowboy-style with corn bread or Mexican refried beans with tortillas, so this rustic fava bean breakfast dish naturally appeals to me. Of course, *ful medames* (as it's known in Egypt) can be enjoyed at any time of day. Salt, lemon juice, and cumin are the traditional seasonings. It is only a little soupy, but best eaten with a spoon nonetheless, accompanied by pita or other flatbreads. Dried fava beans can be found in Middle Eastern groceries.

SERVES 4 TO 6

1 pound small dried peeled fava beans

1 small onion, halved

8 cups water

2 teaspoons cumin seeds

Salt and pepper

4 garlic cloves, minced

¼ cup olive oil

2 small ripe tomatoes, chopped

¼ cup chopped red onion

4 hard-cooked eggs (or fried eggs,
 if preferred)

Lemon wedges

Put the beans in a medium heavy pot, add the onion and water, and bring to a boil over high heat. Turn down the heat to a gentle simmer and skim any rising foam. Cook until the beans are tender and falling apart, about 1 hour.

Meanwhile, toast the cumin seeds in a small dry pan over medium-high heat until fragrant, about 1 minute. Coarsely grind in a spice mill or with a mortar and pestle.

Remove the halved onion from the pot and discard. Season the beans with salt and pepper. Add the garlic and olive oil and simmer for 15 minutes, or until quite thick. Mash the beans a bit if you like.

Spoon the beans into bowls and garnish with the tomatoes, chopped onion, and eggs. Sprinkle with salt and the toasted cumin. Serve with lemon wedges.

fresh shell beans with rosemary gremolata

Fresh shell beans are a fleeting treat, usually available only in summer months. Look for cranberry beans or other varieties like fresh butter beans, sold in the pod at farmers' markets. Some growers sell them already shelled. Unlike their dried cousins, fresh shell beans need only about 30 minutes to become tender and creamy. You can eat them warm or at room temperature, with a drizzle of good olive oil and a sprinkling of salt. Or try them this way, with a sprightly mixture of parsley, rosemary, lemon zest, and garlic. They're also good with a spoonful of Mrs. Paganelli's "Pesto" (page 102). SERVES 4

2 pounds fresh shell beans, shelled
(about 2 cups)

4 garlic cloves

Salt

2 tablespoons olive oil, plus more for
drizzling

1 teaspoon finely chopped rosemary

3 tablespoons finely chopped parsley

Grated zest of ½ lemon

1 garlic clove, finely minced

Put the shelled beans in a small pot, cover with 4 cups water, and add the garlic cloves, a generous pinch of salt, and the olive oil. Bring to a boil, then reduce the heat to a simmer and cook for 30 minutes.

Check to see if the beans are soft, tender, and creamy throughout; if necessary, continue to cook for a little longer. If they are not to be served immediately, let the beans cool in their broth and then reheat later.

To serve, drain the warm beans (save the broth for soup) and put them in a bowl. Mix together the rosemary, parsley, lemon zest, and the minced garlic and sprinkle over the beans. Add a drizzle of olive oil.

rice porridge with salted egg

In Southeast Asia, rice porridge is commonly eaten for breakfast, but need I say it's good at midnight too? You may be inclined to skip the salted eggs, but they really are sensational and worth trying. Otherwise, just stir a roughly beaten egg into the soup at the last minute and let it quickly cook into strands. Top the *jook,* as this porridge is called in Malaysia, with fried shallots and chiles, slivered scallions, and a few drops of sesame oil.   SERVES 4

1 cup jasmine or other long-grain white rice

6 to 7 cups chicken broth or water

Salt

4 Salted Eggs (optional; recipe follows)

Vegetable oil for deep-frying

3 large shallots, sliced into 1/8-inch-thick rings

12 small dried red chile peppers

Soy sauce

2 scallions, thinly slivered

Toasted sesame oil

Wash the rice well several times in cold water. Put it in a medium heavy pot, add the broth and a teaspoon of salt, and bring to a boil. Turn the heat to a low simmer and cook, stirring occasionally, for 20 minutes. Add the salted eggs, if using. Cook for 10 to 15 minutes more: the rice grains will swell and become quite soft but should still remain discernible.

Meanwhile, to make the fried shallot garnish, pour vegetable oil to a level of 1 inch in a wok or skillet and heat to about 350°F. Add the sliced shallots and chiles and fry until the shallots are crisp and golden, about 3 to 4 minutes. Drain on paper towels and sprinkle with salt.

To serve, season the porridge to taste with salt and soy sauce. Retrieve the salted eggs, if used, from the pot, peel, and roughly chop.

CONTINUED

Ladle the porridge into bowls, add a spoonful of chopped egg, and sprinkle with the fried shallots and chiles. Garnish each bowl with some slivered scallions and a little drizzle of sesame oil.

salted eggs

MAKES 12 EGGS

Dissolve 2 cups kosher salt in 8 cups cold water, whisk well, and pour into a large jar or other nonreactive container. Carefully submerge a dozen eggs in the brine. The salted eggs can be stored, refrigerated, for up to 3 months, but are ready to use after 2 weeks. Cook for 10 to 15 minutes and use to garnish the rice porridge.

mexican corn and squash blossom soup

This soup reminds me of an ethereal one I had many years ago in Oaxaca, made entirely of bright yellow squash flowers (you could buy an armload of them there for just a few pesos). To get your hands on enough squash blossoms to make that same soup here, you'd need a large vegetable garden or have to pay a small fortune at the farmers' market. So I've adapted the recipe, adding corn and summer squash as well. The essence of squash blossom still prevails, and the soup still has its heady flavor and velvety texture.

SERVES 4 TO 6

4 tablespoons butter

1 cup diced onion

3 cups sweet corn kernels (from about 4 ears)

1 pound yellow summer squash, cut into ½-inch chunks

Salt and pepper

¼ cup long-grain white rice

4 cups chicken broth, or as needed

½ pound squash blossoms, cut into ½-inch slices

Grated nutmeg

In a medium heavy pot, melt the butter over medium heat. Add the onion and cook until softened, about 5 minutes. Add the corn kernels and squash and season well with salt and pepper. Add the rice and chicken broth, bring to a simmer, and simmer gently for about 15 minutes, until the rice is tender.

Add the squash blossoms and cook for 5 minutes more.

Puree the soup in a blender, in batches if necessary, then pass through a fine-mesh strainer into a large saucepan. Thin with a little more broth or water if necessary, and adjust the seasoning. Reheat and add a little freshly grated nutmeg.

clams in the shell
with fennel and parsley

It has always been incredible to me that just a few dozen clams in a pot with some aromatics can produce such an abundance of delicious broth, and I marvel at the mystery of it. How? Never mind, I'll happily enjoy a steaming bowlful any time. Though some would add a twirl of al dente spaghetti or linguine, for me it is the fragrant, briny broth that delights—better with a crusty loaf and a spoon.

The smallest clams are the most tender. Look for littlenecks on the East Coast, or Manila clams from the Pacific. **SERVES 2**

2 tablespoons olive oil

1 small onion, finely diced

1 medium leek, trimmed and
  finely diced

Salt and pepper

1 teaspoon crushed fennel seeds

2 garlic cloves, minced

Pinch of red pepper flakes

2 pounds small clams, like littlenecks
  or Manila, scrubbed

Splash of white wine

2 tablespoons chopped parsley

1 tablespoon chopped scallion

Lemon wedges

In a wide deep pot, heat the olive oil over medium-high heat. Add the onion and leek and cook, stirring occasionally, until softened, about 5 minutes.

Season with salt and pepper, then add the fennel seeds, garlic, and red pepper flakes. Add the clams, turn the heat to high, and stir well with a wooden spoon to coat. Splash in the wine, put on the lid, and cook until all the clams have opened, 5 to 6 minutes.

Stir in the parsley and scallions. Spoon the clams and broth into bowls. Serve with lemon wedges.

polentina alla toscana

Some soups, once encountered, live on in both memory and a cook's personal repertoire. This very traditional Tuscan soup impressed me when I first encountered it in Florence. I loved the way a little polenta could be used to thicken, ever so slightly, a vegetable soup. There was something special too about the deep, dark kale and fruity olive oil that were added to the bowl. My version is faithful to the original, so good that there was no need to embroider. SERVES 4 TO 6

¼ cup extra virgin olive oil, plus more
  (optional) for drizzling

1 large onion, diced

½ pound carrots, peeled and diced

4 celery stalks, diced

1 large fennel bulb, trimmed and diced

Salt and pepper

1 medium leek, trimmed and cut into
  ½-inch squares

1 bay leaf

¼ cup polenta

6 cups chicken broth

½ pound kale, preferably Tuscan

½ teaspoon grated or finely chopped
  garlic

Pinch of red pepper flakes

Leaves from 1 rosemary sprig

In a heavy pot, heat 2 tablespoons of the olive oil over medium-high heat. Add the onion, carrots, celery, and fennel, season generously with salt and pepper, and cook, stirring, for 5 minutes or so, until barely softened. Add the leek and bay leaf and cook for 2 minutes.

Add the polenta, stirring to distribute it, and raise the heat to high. Add the chicken broth and bring to a boil, then reduce the heat to a gentle simmer and allow the soup to simmer for about an hour; the broth should be just slightly thickened. Taste and adjust the seasoning.

CONTINUED

Meanwhile, wash and roughly chop the kale. Drain in a colander but do not dry. Heat the remaining 2 tablespoons olive oil in a wide skillet over high heat. When the oil is hot, add the greens, stirring as they begin to wilt. Add the garlic and red pepper flakes and season with salt and pepper. Turn the heat to medium, cover, and cook until the greens are tender, about 5 minutes more. Set aside.

To serve, ladle the soup into bowls and top with the kale. Sprinkle with the chopped rosemary (finely chop it at the last minute), and drizzle with more olive oil if desired.

semolina and ricotta gnocchi

To make these gnocchi, I use fine semolina flour, ground from hard yellow wheat, which has a distinctive nutty, sweet flavor, and employ an old-fashioned method, similar to making French pâte à choux, the pastry used to make cream puffs or gougères. The semolina flour is first cooked in water with a little butter until it forms a ball, the eggs are beaten into the dough and then fresh ricotta and a little sharp Pecorino cheese are added. Unlike conventional potato gnocchi, the dough is not rolled; rather, it is dropped by spoonfuls into a pot of boiling water. The gnocchi are well-seasoned, tender, and light and can be served in either a savory homemade broth or in a pool of sage-infused butter. They can also be cooked ahead, then baked in an earthenware dish with a handful of Parmesan. MAKES ABOUT 40 GNOCCHI; SERVES 4 TO 6

2 cups water

6 tablespoons butter

1 cup fine semolina flour

3 large eggs

Salt and pepper

Grated nutmeg

½ teaspoon grated lemon zest

½ cup fresh ricotta, drained

½ cup grated Pecorino Romano
   cheese, plus more (optional) for
   garnish

2 teaspoons finely chopped sage

2 tablespoons slivered chives or
   scallions

6 tablespoons butter, melted, or 6 cups
   well-seasoned hot chicken broth

12 large sage leaves, for garnish

1 tablespoon chopped flat-leaf parsley
   (optional)

Put the water in a medium saucepan, add the 6 tablespoons solid butter, and bring to a boil. Reduce the heat to medium-high, add the semolina all at once, and stir vigorously with a wooden spoon until it comes together in a ball; this will take a minute or two. Cook for a minute more, until firm.

Transfer the dough to the bowl of a stand mixer fitted with the paddle attachment (alternatively, use a handheld mixer). Beat the dough at medium speed for a few minutes, until it has cooled slightly and given off its steam. Now begin adding the eggs one at a time, making sure you have completely incorporated each egg before adding the next one; increase the speed if necessary. The final dough should look smooth and glossy. Mix in 1/2 teaspoon salt and a generous amount of pepper, then add nutmeg to taste, the lemon zest, ricotta, Pecorino, chopped sage, and chives, and mix on medium speed for a minute or two to combine the ingredients.

To cook the gnocchi, bring a large wide pot of salted water to a rapid simmer. With a teaspoon, scoop up walnut-sized pieces of dough and nudge them into the water with the help of a second spoon. Cook about 12 gnocchi at a time so as not to overcrowd. When they rise to the surface, let them simmer for 2 minutes, then transfer to a warm bowl with a spider or a slotted spoon. Repeat with the remaining gnocchi.

Warm the melted butter in a small skillet over medium heat, add the sage leaves, and simmer for 1 minute.

Divide the gnocchi among shallow soup bowls. Drizzle the gnocchi generously with the sage-infused butter. Sprinkle some cheese and parsley over each bowl, if desired.

Alternatively, if serving in broth (4 gnocchi per bowl is sufficient), add the sage leaves to the broth when heating. Ladle the broth over the gnocchi and serve with cheese and parsley. Baked gnocchi may also be served with either the sage-infused butter or the broth.

very green fish stew

I wanted this simple fish stew to be especially herbaceous, so I used lots of cilantro, basil, and mint, along with the pungent flavors of lemongrass, chiles, and ginger. For tropical sweetness, I added both coconut and coconut oil. The resulting broth is bright, spicy, satisfying, and most definitely green. The green sauce could also be stirred into a pot of steamed clams or mussels.

SERVES 4

PHOTOGRAPH ON PAGE 110

FOR THE GREEN SAUCE
(MAKES ABOUT 1 CUP)
1 cup cilantro leaves and tender stems
   (about 2 ounces)
1 cup basil leaves (about 2 ounces)
¼ cup mint leaves (about ½ ounce)
A 2-inch piece of fresh ginger, peeled
   and thickly sliced
2 garlic cloves
2 small serrano or fresh Thai chiles,
   chopped
½ cup grated unsweetened coconut
   (fresh, dried, or frozen)
A 4-inch length of lemongrass, tender
   center only, sliced ¼ inch thick

2 teaspoons fish sauce
2 teaspoons brown sugar
½ teaspoon salt
Ice water (optional)

1½ pounds firm white-fleshed fish
   fillet, cut into 1-inch chunks
Salt and pepper
2 tablespoons coconut or vegetable oil
2 cups chicken broth, vegetable broth,
   or water
3 or 4 scallions, thinly sliced
Lime wedges

To make the green sauce, put the cilantro, basil, mint, ginger, garlic, chiles, coconut, lemongrass, fish sauce, sugar, and salt in a blender or food processor. Quickly process to make a smooth, thick puree, adding a little ice water if necessary. Taste and adjust the seasoning; it should be quite spicy.

Season the fish chunks lightly with salt and pepper. Heat the oil in a wide deep pan over medium heat. Add the fish and fry lightly for 1 minute on one side. Flip the fish and raise the heat to medium-high. Add the broth and half of the green sauce, then put on the lid and cook for 2 minutes, or just until the fish is opaque throughout. Gently stir in the remaining green sauce. Taste the broth and adjust the salt if necessary. Ladle the stew into bowls, sprinkle with the scallions, and serve with lime wedges.

tunisian meatballs

In France, meatballs are called *boulettes* (sounds better than "meatballs," *non*?), and by far the most popular versions are the spice-scented North African type. In Morocco, Tunisia, and Algeria, former French colonies, that's also what meatballs are called, at least on tourist menus. They are simmered in a spice-laden, saffron-scented sauce, with just enough hot pepper to keep it interesting. Served with steaming-hot buttered couscous, these nearly bite-size, tender *boulettes* make a warming, comforting meal. Fear not: although the ingredients list is long, this is really a very simple recipe, parts of which can be prepared in advance. SERVES 4 TO 6

FOR THE SAUCE

2 tablespoons olive oil

1½ cups finely diced onions

3 garlic cloves, minced

2 tablespoons tomato paste

A 1-inch piece of cinnamon stick

Large pinch of saffron, crumbled

Salt and pepper

3 cups chicken broth, vegetable broth,
   or water

FOR THE MEATBALLS

1½ cups cubed day-old firm white
   bread

1 cup milk

1 pound ground beef or lamb

1 large egg, beaten

4 garlic cloves, minced

1 teaspoon salt

¼ teaspoon pepper

2 teaspoons paprika

1 teaspoon ground ginger

1 teaspoon turmeric

½ teaspoon ground cumin

¼ teaspoon cayenne

¼ teaspoon ground cloves

¼ teaspoon ground coriander

⅛ teaspoon grated nutmeg

2 tablespoons chopped parsley, plus
   1 tablespoon for garnish

2 tablespoons chopped cilantro, plus
   1 tablespoon for garnish

2 tablespoons finely chopped scallions,
   plus 1 tablespoon for garnish

All-purpose flour for dusting

Olive or vegetable oil for shallow-frying

CONTINUED

FOR THE COUSCOUS

1 cup giant couscous, medium couscous, or m'hamsa

2 tablespoons butter

½ cup golden raisins, soaked in hot water until softened, then drained

Salt

¼ teaspoon ground cinnamon

To make the sauce, heat the oil in a wide heavy saucepan over medium-high heat. Add the onions and cook, without browning, until softened, about 5 minutes. Add the garlic, tomato paste, cinnamon stick, and saffron and stir well to incorporate. Season generously with salt and pepper and allow to sizzle for 1 minute. Add the broth, bring to a simmer, and simmer gently for 10 minutes. Remove from the heat. The sauce can be made up to a day in advance and refrigerated.

To make the meatballs, put the bread cubes and milk in a small bowl and let the bread soak until softened, about 5 minutes, then squeeze dry and transfer to a medium bowl.

Add the ground meat to the bread and mix gently with your hands, then add the egg, garlic, salt, pepper, paprika, ginger, turmeric, cumin, cayenne, cloves, coriander, and nutmeg, and mix well to distribute the seasonings. Add 2 tablespoons each of the parsley, cilantro, and scallions and knead for a minute. The meat mixture can be prepared up to a day in advance and refrigerated.

With your hands, roll the meat mixture into small balls about the size of a quarter. Dust lightly with flour. Heat ¼ inch of oil in a wide heavy skillet over medium-high heat. Fry the meatballs, turning once, until barely browned, about 2 minutes per side. Drain and blot on paper towels.

Add the meatballs to the sauce, bring to a simmer over medium heat, cover, and cook for about 20 minutes, until the sauce has thickened slightly and the meatballs are tender. Taste the sauce and adjust the seasoning, adding salt or cayenne as necessary.

Meanwhile, cook the couscous according to the package directions, then fluff gently and stir in the butter and raisins. Season with salt and the cinnamon and toss well.

Spoon the couscous into shallow bowls and top with the meatballs and plenty of sauce. Garnish with the remaining parsley, cilantro, and scallions.

NOTE: Regarding the browning of the meatballs, dusting them in flour before lightly frying helps keep them tender and thickens the sauce, but they can be browned without flour if desired. Or, instead of frying, they can be briefly broiled before simmering. And if you don't want the sauce, just finish the cooking in the skillet and serve the panfried meatballs crisp and hot.

winter minestrone

This is not a vegetable-laden summer minestrone. It's mostly about earthy, creamy, slowly cooked white beans with accents of pancetta, roasted winter squash, and rosemary. Choose sweet, firm-fleshed squashes like kabocha, delicata, or butternut. SERVES 4 TO 6

3 tablespoons olive oil

2 medium onions, cut into small dice

Salt and pepper

1/4 pound pancetta or bacon, sliced into 1/4-inch-wide strips

3 garlic cloves, minced

1/2 teaspoon crushed fennel seeds

1/4 teaspoon red pepper flakes

1 pound dried cannellini beans, soaked overnight in cold water and drained

6 cups water

1 pound winter squash, peeled and cut into 1/2-inch cubes

1/2 pound small pasta, such as tubetti or orrechiette, cooked until al dente and drained

2 teaspoons chopped rosemary

Fruity olive oil for drizzling

In a heavy soup pot, heat 2 tablespoons of the olive oil over medium-high heat. Add the onions, season with salt, and cook until softened, about 5 minutes. Add the pancetta, garlic, fennel seeds, and red pepper flakes and cook for 2 minutes. Add the beans and water, bring to a simmer, and cook gently until the beans are very tender, about 1½ hours.

Meanwhile, heat the oven to 400°F. Put the squash cubes on a baking sheet, season with salt and pepper, and coat with the remaining tablespoon olive oil. Roast until tender and lightly caramelized, about 30 minutes. Set aside to cool. Adjust the seasoning of the beans and broth with salt and pepper. Gently stir in the cooked squash and pasta and heat through.

To serve, ladle into bowls. Sprinkle each serving with a pinch of freshly chopped rosemary and a drizzle of fruity olive oil.

Fresh turnips (left) and Young Turnips, Greens and All (page 153)

VEGETABLES TO SAVOR

steaming, braising, and wilting

I have always loved, loved, loved vegetables, even as a child. In my mother's kitchen, however, they were usually a colorful mixture in a frozen chunk. Sometimes they were even canned (frozen was a significantly better option, I thought). But nobody had to force me to eat my spinach. To this day, cooked greens are often my favorite part of the meal. In this chapter you'll find a number of heavenly examples, from barely wilted arugula to Japanese chrysanthemum and long-cooked kale. I find it fascinating that every type of cooking green has a distinct flavor and personality, yet all are delicious and healthful.

There are all kinds of vegetables here to glorify and praise, and most of them are quite humble. Onions, cabbage, carrots, and leeks are not very glamorous; still, I find them exciting. Turnips make me smile, especially young ones. I also get excited about legumes—peas and beans, fresh or dry—and about lentils, in a salad or soup. Freshly dug new potatoes are a real turn-on. A cheap thrill perhaps, but a thrill nonetheless. Any of the following dishes can certainly be considered as an accompaniment to a main course, but sitting down to a supper (or a snack) of vegetables alone can be quite satisfying.

south indian cabbage with black mustard seeds

Ordinary green cabbage can be transformed by a bright, spicy combination of Indian aromatics. This fresh-tasting stir-fry may well make you a cabbage lover in spite of yourself. It makes a great side dish, since it goes with almost everything. It's also quite satisfying served just with plain steamed basmati rice and a spoonful of yogurt raita. You can treat Brussels sprouts the same way. SERVES 4

2 tablespoons ghee, clarified butter, or vegetable oil

1 teaspoon black mustard seeds

½ teaspoon cumin seeds

½ teaspoon grated garlic

½ teaspoon grated ginger

1 teaspoon finely chopped serrano or other green chile

¼ teaspoon turmeric

1 pound firm green cabbage, quartered, cored, and sliced ⅛ inch thick

Salt and pepper

Juice of ½ lime

Heat the ghee in a large wok or a wide skillet over medium-high heat. Add the mustard and cumin seeds and let them sizzle. When they begin to pop, add the garlic, ginger, chile, and turmeric, then quickly add the cabbage and stir to coat. Season with salt and pepper and stir-fry until the cabbage wilts slightly, about 5 minutes.

Finish with a squeeze or two of lime juice and transfer to a serving dish.

warm french lentil salad

In cold weather, there's something completely pleasurable about a warm, savory French lentil salad. And when I say French, I don't just mean in the French manner (though this salad is)—you really need to use French lentils. They keep their shape when cooked, and their firm, nutty texture holds up to the acid in an assertive dressing. Ordinary brown supermarket lentils are fine for soup, but for a good lentil salad, you want those beautiful little imported gray-green lentilles du Puy. They cook in about 30 minutes.

Dress the warm lentils with the garlicky mustard vinaigrette, add thick slices of smoked pork belly and boiled fingerling potatoes, and sprinkle with lots of chopped scallions and parsley. A magnificent meal. SERVES 4 TO 6

¾ pound smoked pork belly or good-quality slab bacon, 1½ to 2 inches thick

1 large onion, halved and each half stuck with a clove

4 thyme branches

1 small carrot, peeled

1 cup small green French lentils, picked over and rinsed

1 small bay leaf

Salt and pepper

1 pound fingerling or other small potatoes, rinsed

FOR THE VINAIGRETTE

1 large shallot, finely diced

2 tablespoons red wine vinegar

2 garlic cloves, smashed to a paste with a little salt

Salt and pepper

1 tablespoon Dijon mustard

¼ cup fruity olive oil

2 teaspoons capers, rinsed and roughly chopped

2 tablespoons chopped cornichons or other sour gherkins

½ cup chopped parsley, plus 1 tablespoon for garnish

¼ cup chopped scallions, plus 1 tablespoon for garnish

CONTINUED

Put the pork belly in a small pot with 1 of the onion halves, 2 of the thyme branches, and the carrot. Add water to cover, bring to a simmer, and cook until the meat is tender, about 45 minutes. Turn off the heat and keep warm in the liquid.

Meanwhile, put the lentils in a saucepan and add the other onion half, the 2 remaining thyme branches, and the bay leaf. Add 4 cups water and a little salt, bring to a simmer, and cook gently until the lentils are firm-tender, 25 to 30 minutes. Drain (discard the onion, thyme, and bay leaf) and keep warm.

Cook the potatoes in their skins in well-salted boiling water until tender, about 15 minutes. Drain and keep warm.

To make the vinaigrette, macerate the shallot in the red wine vinegar in a small bowl for 5 minutes.

Add the garlic, a pinch each of salt and pepper, and the mustard to the shallot, then whisk in the olive oil to make a thick dressing. Stir in the chopped capers and cornichons. Just before serving, stir in the ½ cup parsley and ¼ cup scallions.

To serve, dress the lentils with half the vinaigrette, then transfer to a platter or serving bowl. Slice the pork belly (or bacon) crosswise into ¼-inch slices (save the broth for soup) and arrange over the lentils. Cut the potatoes lengthwise in half and arrange cut side up around the pork. Spoon the remaining vinaigrette over the sliced meat and potatoes and sprinkle with the remaining 1 tablespoon each scallions and parsley.

NOTE: This vinaigrette is also great with boiled or roasted beef, hot or cold, as well as with boiled or steamed vegetables, like leeks.

young turnips, greens and all

Larger turnips, the kind sold loose, are good roasted, which concentrates their sweetness and gives them a wonderfully browned crisp exterior. But for this dish, which celebrates young greens, you want baby turnips, the smaller the better, sold in bunches with their fresh leafy tops still attached. Since the turnips take a little longer to cook than the greens, begin by steaming them in a small amount of water and a bit of butter, then toss in the tender greens for a quick minute or two.   SERVES 4

PHOTOGRAPH ON PAGE 146

2 bunches young turnips with greens (about 2 pounds)	2 tablespoons butter or olive oil
	Salt and pepper

Cut the greens from the turnips, leaving a bit of stem attached to each turnip. Wash twice in cold water, then drain. Roughly chop the greens or, if they are quite small, leave them whole. Set aside.

Trim the roots from the turnips with a paring knife. Unless they are very small, halve or quarter the turnips. Soak in a bowl of water to remove any grit.

Put the butter in a large saucepan, add the turnips, and season with salt and pepper. Add ½ cup water and bring to a simmer over medium-high heat. Cover and let steam until the turnips are tender, about 3 minutes. Add the turnip greens and a pinch more salt and continue cooking, covered, to wilt the greens, about a minute more.

classic frisée salad

If Cobb salad is quintessentially American, then *frisée aux lardons* is its French counterpart. Both have immense popularity, and both have bacon and eggs. The main ingredient of the latter is curly endive (frisée), of which the French are inordinately fond. Curly endive is the mildest member of the chicory family, and aside from beauty (a head of frisée is indeed a sight to behold), its virtue is the ability to stand up to an assertive dressing. When preparing this salad, take care to remove the tough outer leaves—it's the tender, blanched pale green interior that you want.   SERVES 4

6 ounces thick-cut bacon, sliced crosswise into 1/4-inch-wide lardons

2 teaspoons Dijon mustard

2 tablespoons sherry vinegar

1/2 teaspoon grated garlic

3 tablespoons extra virgin olive oil

Salt and pepper

4 eggs

4 handfuls tender, pale frisée (about 10 ounces)

12 thin slices baguette, lightly toasted and rubbed with a garlic clove

Simmer the bacon in a small amount of water for about 5 minutes. Drain. In a small skillet, cook the bacon over medium heat (no need to add oil) until lightly browned and crisp but still a bit springy. Blot on a paper towel.

Meanwhile, for the vinaigrette, whisk together the mustard, vinegar, and garlic in a small bowl. Whisk in the olive oil. Season with salt and pepper.

Fill a shallow skillet two-thirds full with salted water and bring to a gentle simmer. Crack the eggs carefully into the water. Poach the eggs for 3 to 4 minutes, until the whites have set but the yolks are still soft. With a slotted spoon, remove to a paper-towel-lined plate. Lightly salt the frisée and toss with the vinaigrette, coating it well. Divide the greens among four plates, place an egg in the center of each, and add 3 baguette toasts. Scatter the lardons over the salads, add a little ground black pepper, and serve.

just-wilted arugula

We think of tender young arugula, with its peppery flavor, as a salad green, which of course it is. Larger-leafed bunches, however, are perfect for cooking. When it is wilted quickly, just as you would treat tender spinach, arugula's characteristic nutty flavor comes through but its sharpness is softened. It takes seconds, not minutes. Use cooked arugula as an easy and delicious side dish, or add it to pasta dishes at the last minute.   SERVES 4

1 tablespoon olive oil or butter

2 garlic cloves, minced

1 pound arugula, rinsed and trimmed but not dried

Salt and pepper

Heat the olive oil in a wide skillet over medium-high heat. Add the garlic and let it sizzle for about 15 seconds without browning. Toss the leaves into the pan, add salt and pepper, and cook, stirring, until just wilted, 30 to 40 seconds.

long-cooked kale, please

Not to sound cranky, but to say that I am baffled by the current craze for eating kale raw is an understatement. And kale chips? Barbecue-flavored? Do enlighten me. On the other hand, cooked kale is wonderful, especially long cooked. In Portugal, fabulous deep-green kale soups are simmered for hours. Here is a recipe for 30-minute kale, but you can cook it even longer. Use *lacinato* (dinosaur) kale if it's available. Serve in bowls with plenty of the delicious broth, good for sopping up with crusty bread. SERVES 4 TO 6

2 pounds kale

3 tablespoons olive oil

2 medium onions, sliced

Salt and pepper

½ pound Spanish chorizo, sliced

½ inch thick, or slab bacon,

cut into ½-inch chunks

Large pinch of red pepper flakes

Sherry vinegar (optional)

Cut the kale crosswise into 2-inch pieces, discarding any tough stems. Wash twice in cold water to remove any grit and drain.

Heat the olive oil in a large heavy pot over medium-high heat. Add the onions, season with salt and pepper, and cook until softened, about 5 minutes; adjust the heat as necessary so the onions don't brown too much. Add the chorizo and red pepper flakes and cook for 2 minutes more.

Add the kale a handful at a time, sprinkling each handful lightly with salt, then turn the heat to high and stir with a wooden spoon to help the greens wilt. Add 1 cup water and continue to stir until it is simmering briskly. Cover and turn the heat to low; it should be rather brothy—add more water if necessary. Cook the kale slowly, stirring occasionally, for about 30 minutes, until very tender.

Taste and adjust the seasoning, adding a few drops of sherry vinegar if desired.

well-charred endives with anchovy butter

Belgian endives can add crisp sweetness to winter salads. Eaten raw, they are not as assertive as some of their chicory relatives, like red radicchio and Treviso. Yet when cooked, endives can sometimes seem unpleasantly bitter. The solution is to brown them quite ruthlessly, until they're nearly burned. The high heat caramelizes and sweetens the endive in a remarkable way.

SERVES 4

4 tablespoons butter, softened

2 teaspoons chopped anchovies

1 garlic clove, smashed to a paste with
    a little salt or grated

½ teaspoon grated lemon zest

1 tablespoon chopped parsley

2 teaspoons thinly slivered chives

Salt and pepper

4 large Belgian endives

1 tablespoon olive oil

Put the butter in a small bowl, add the anchovies, garlic, lemon zest, parsley, and chives, and mix well. Season with salt and pepper and set aside.

Cut the endives lengthwise in half, discarding any tough outer leaves, and trim a bit off the stem end. Season on both sides with salt and pepper.

Heat the broiler. Heat the olive oil in a wide cast-iron skillet over medium-high heat. When the oil is hot, lay the endive cut side down in the pan and let brown for 3 or 4 minutes. Turn the endive over and cook for 2 minutes more.

Put the pan under the broiler and leave until the endive is well browned and beginning to char. Serve warm, smeared with the anchovy butter.

steamed new potatoes
with aromatics

A friend in the South of France once served me new potatoes that had been steamed over a huge bed of wild thyme branches, a lovely way to cook them. Back home I use this method: put the unpeeled potatoes in a wide pot with an inch or two of water, then add a handful of aromatic herbs and spices. Over a high flame, the small potatoes cook quickly in a fragrant, steamy bath. Now, will it be sweet butter? fruity olive oil? or crème fraîche? SERVES 4 TO 6

2 pounds new potatoes, 1½ to 2 inches
   in diameter
1 small bunch thyme
A few rosemary sprigs
4 bay leaves

¼ teaspoon black peppercorns
1 head garlic, separated into cloves but
   not peeled
Salt

Scrub the potatoes but do not peel. Put the thyme, rosemary, bay leaves, peppercorns, and garlic cloves in a wide heavy pot. Add the potatoes in one layer and enough water to barely cover. Sprinkle with a generous amount of salt, about 2 teaspoons. Put on the lid and bring to a hard boil. Reduce the heat slightly to maintain a rapid simmer and cook, covered, for about 15 minutes. Check the potatoes with a skewer to make sure they have cooked through.

Turn off the heat and leave the potatoes for at least 10 minutes, or up to half an hour. To serve, drain the potatoes and put them in a serving bowl, with the aromatics still clinging to them.

steamed asian greens

On menus in Chinese restaurants, there's always an item on the English side called "Green Vegetable." When I see plates sailing by to other tables piled with the most brilliant greens, I can't help but order some. In fact, I am always heading to Chinatown to buy them for cooking at home. I admire the merchants, usually female, who take such great pride in their trade. They make such beautifully displayed rows of colorful greens, like Chinese morning glory (water spinach), tiny bok choy, and flowering mustard. SERVES 4

2 tablespoons vegetable oil

3 or 4 small dried red chile peppers

2 teaspoons grated ginger

2 teaspoons grated garlic

1½ pounds small bok choy or Chinese
    morning glory, tough stems removed

Salt

1 teaspoon soy sauce

½ teaspoon toasted sesame oil

In a large wok or a wide skillet, heat the oil over high heat. Add the chiles, ginger, and garlic and let sizzle, without browning. Add the greens, sprinkle lightly with salt, and stir to coat. Add a splash of water, and put on the lid. The steam created in the closed vessel will cook most greens in a minute or two. Finish with a drizzle of the soy sauce and sesame oil.

slow-roasted tomatoes

Stewed tomatoes, an old-fashioned side dish, can be wonderful but are a little fussy to make. Instead, I begin with the ripest summer tomatoes, peeled or not (I usually don't), and slow-roast them in olive oil perfumed with garlic and herbs. As they cook, their sweetness is concentrated. These tomatoes are wonderful served warm or at room temperature with grilled fish—no other sauce needed. I also like them cold the next day with a few slices of mozzarella, a dab of fresh ricotta, or some crumbled feta. SERVES 6 TO 8

6 large, ripe tomatoes

Salt and pepper

Olive oil

4 garlic cloves, sliced

A handful of basil leaves

Heat the oven to 350°F. Core the tomatoes, cut them in half, and season the cut halves with salt and pepper. Place the tomatoes cut side up in a shallow earthenware baking dish in one layer. Pour about 1 cup olive oil evenly over the tomato halves, and scatter the garlic and basil leaves over, tucking them in here and there. Bake, uncovered, for about 45 minutes, basting with oil occasionally. The tomatoes should hold their shape, but barely. Leave them in the olive oil for 30 minutes before serving or let them cool to room temperature.

NOTE: Use the fragrant leftover oil to make salad dressings or for cooking vegetables.

braised lettuce and sweet peas

If your great-great-grandmother was French or British, she would have known how to braise lettuce. Although braised lettuce was once a rather common dish, it's rarely seen in the twenty-first century. To me, the concept still has great appeal, but it's best when the lettuce is cooked just until tender. Add sweet peas if you are making this in the spring or summer; otherwise, skip them and just add the herbs. Any kind of sturdy head will work for this dish: Little Gem or romaine lettuce is a good choice.   SERVES 4 TO 6

6 Little Gem lettuces or 2 small heads
    romaine

2 tablespoons butter

1 medium onion, diced

Salt and pepper

½ cup chopped ham

1 cup shelled peas

½ cup chicken broth or water

1 tablespoon chopped parsley

1 tablespoon chopped mint

If using Little Gem lettuces, trim the bottoms and discard the tough outer leaves. Cut lengthwise in half, rinse briefly, and drain. If using romaine, cut the heads into quarters.

In a wide large skillet, melt the butter over medium-high heat. Add the onion, season with salt and pepper, and cook until softened, about 5 minutes. Add the ham, peas, and broth, and bring to a simmer. Add the lettuces in one layer and sprinkle lightly with salt. Put on the lid and let steam for about 5 minutes, until the lettuce is tender.

Stir in the chopped parsley and mint.

broccoli rabe, italian-style

This green vegetable is known by many names. Italians call it cime di rapa, rapini, or raab. It's most often seen in American markets labeled broccoli rabe. Its flavor is clear and distinctive—a hint of bitterness and a deep, mustardy sweetness. Broccoli rabe cries out for aggressive seasoning, fairly begging for olive oil, hot red pepper (peperoncino), garlic, rosemary, and fennel seed. I could eat a huge pile all by itself, or with a fine companion like cannellini beans or a slice of roast pork. Note that you can blanch the greens well ahead of time, then finish and season them just before serving.

SERVES 4 TO 6

Salt and pepper

2 pounds broccoli rabe

2 tablespoons olive oil

3 garlic cloves, minced

Large pinch of red pepper flakes

½ teaspoon chopped rosemary

½ teaspoon crushed fennel seeds

Lemon wedges

Bring a large pot of well-salted water to a boil. Meanwhile, cut the broccoli rabe into 2-inch pieces, including the tender stems.

Wilt the rabe slightly by plunging it into the boiling water for 1 minute. Drain and spread out on a baking sheet to cool (you can do this several hours ahead).

In a wide skillet, heat the olive oil over medium-high heat. Add the garlic, red pepper flakes, rosemary, and fennel seeds and let sizzle without browning. Add the rabe and stir well to coat, then season with salt and pepper and cook for about 2 minutes, until heated through. Serve warm or at room temperature, with lemon wedges.

chrysanthemum greens with silken tofu

I'm a fan of good old-fashioned creamed spinach, but this light-handed varia-tion, with no butter or cream in sight, can be even more satisfying. It employs tender chrysanthemum leaves, which have a curious floral flavor and a slight tannic edge. Of course, you need to use cultivated edible chrysanthemum greens, not the plants grown for their showy flowers. Use spinach if you can't find chrysanthemum, but it's worth searching out. When briefly wilted, then combined with soft, custardy tofu, the greens make a delicate treat, best served in small portions. Look for both in a Japanese grocery. SERVES 4

Salt and pepper

2 teaspoons toasted sesame oil

1 teaspoon grated ginger

½ teaspoon sugar

1 teaspoon rice wine

1 pound chrysanthemum greens, tough stems trimmed

¼ pound silken tofu, cut into ½-inch cubes

1 teaspoon toasted sesame seeds

2 tablespoons thinly slivered scallions

2 tablespoons bonito flakes (optional)

Bring a medium pot of well-salted water to a boil.

Meanwhile, make the dressing: whisk together the sesame oil, ginger, sugar, and rice wine. Add the chrysanthemum greens to the boiling water and let soften for 10 seconds. Drain and immediately transfer to a serving bowl. Season lightly with salt and pepper and add the dressing. Stir in the tofu and toss gently.

Sprinkle with the sesame seeds, scallions, and bonito flakes, if using. Serve hot or cold.

swiss chard al forno

Although it's chock-full of vitamins and minerals, chard's main virtue is its extraordinary flavor, which, alas, is practically impossible to describe. Bolder than spinach, yet deeper, sturdier, earthier, and more pure? Versatile too, and a boon to soups, among many other dishes. Chard could almost be considered two vegetables, as the lush leafy greens must be prepared one way and the firm stalks quite another. Here I combine both leaves and stalks in a gratin bound with a light béchamel and a generous sprinkling of Parmesan or Pecorino cheese. Baked until beautifully browned and crisp, it is rather like a lasagna without pasta. SERVES 6

FOR THE BÉCHAMEL
4 tablespoons butter
1/4 cup all-purpose flour
2 to 3 cups milk
Salt and pepper
Grated nutmeg

2 pounds Swiss chard
Salt and pepper
2 tablespoons olive oil
2 garlic cloves, minced
Pinch of red pepper flakes
3 tablespoons butter
3/4 cup grated Parmigano-Reggiano,
    Pecorino Romano, or Gruyère
    cheese

To make the béchamel, melt the 4 tablespoons butter in a small saucepan over medium heat. Whisk in the flour and let cook for 1 minute. Add 2 cups milk, 1/4 cup at a time, whisking constantly as the sauce thickens. Thin with more milk if necessary. Season generously with salt and pepper and with nutmeg to taste. Turn the heat to low and cook, whisking, for 10 to 15 minutes. Keep the sauce warm in a double boiler.

CONTINUED

Meanwhile, cut the stems from the chard. Trim them and cut into batons about ½ inch thick by 3 inches. Rinse well and set aside. Stack the chard leaves about 6 at a time, roll them up like a cigar, and cut into 1-inch-wide strips. Wash twice in cold water and drain.

Bring 8 cups well-salted water to a boil in a saucepan. Add the chard stem batons and simmer until tender, about 5 minutes. Drain and let cool.

Heat the olive oil in a wide skillet over medium-high heat. Add the garlic and red pepper flakes and let sizzle without browning, then add the chopped chard leaves. Season with salt and pepper and stir-fry until just wilted, about 2 minutes. Drain in a colander. When the chard is cool, squeeze to remove excess liquid.

Heat the oven to 400°F. Use 1 tablespoon of the butter to grease a 2-quart gratin dish or shallow baking dish. Add the chard leaves in an even layer. Arrange the cooked stems over the top. Spoon the béchamel over the entire dish. Sprinkle with the grated cheese and dot with the remaining 2 table-spoons butter.

Bake until golden and bubbling, about 25 minutes.

vegetable pot-au-feu

Here's an iconic dish you'll never find in a restaurant—nor, for that matter, in many home kitchens anymore. I learned it from a French grandmother who learned it from her French grandmother. She called it *jardinière* (for the vegetable garden—after all, it contains, but is not limited to, onions, potatoes, carrots, leeks, turnips, and peas). Think of it as a kind of pot-au-feu, so good it doesn't really need meat. You start with a base of onions, then add each successive vegetable according to its cooking time, finishing with a handful of peas. Simmering them all together, along with a good knob of butter, a little bacon, and a bit of broth, makes the whole dish far greater than the sum of its ingredients.   SERVES 4

¼ pound thick-sliced bacon or
   pancetta

6 tablespoons butter

4 small onions, quartered

1 bay leaf

1 large thyme sprig

1 pound Yukon Gold or other yellow-
   fleshed potatoes, peeled and cut into
   2-inch chunks

½ pound medium carrots, peeled and
   cut in half

Salt and pepper

1 medium leek, trimmed and cut into
   1-inch slices

8 small turnips, about 2 inches in
   diameter, peeled and quartered

1 cup shelled peas

Cut the bacon into ½-inch-wide lardons. Put them in a small pot, cover with water, and simmer for 2 minutes, then drain.

Melt the butter in a large wide heavy pot (enameled cast-iron is ideal) over medium heat. Add the bacon and onions, turn up the heat to medium-high, and cook, stirring well for a minute or so. Add the bay leaf, thyme sprig, potatoes, and carrots and stir to coat. Season with salt and pepper. Add 1 cup water and bring to a brisk simmer. Put on the lid and cook, adjusting the heat if necessary, for 15 minutes, or until the potatoes are just done.

Gently stir in the leek and turnips and add a little salt and, if the pot seems to be getting dry, a splash of water. Replace the lid and cook for 5 to 8 minutes more, until the turnips are tender. Add the peas and cook: they will need only a minute or two. Make sure to spoon some of the pot juices over each serving.

STRIKE WHILE THE IRON IS HOT

scorched, seared, and griddled

Although a certain variety of pots and pans is necessary in any home kitchen, the pans I reach for most frequently are made of iron. I have a habit of searching for vintage iron pots at flea markets, and by now I have a rather large collection. It includes cast-iron skillets in several sizes, a wok or two, a large griddle, a Dutch oven, a ridged stovetop grilling pan, a couple of handmade Indian *karahis,* a *comal* from Mexico, and a trusty two-handled French sauté pan that gets daily use. (For high-acid sauces and stews, I recommend enamel-coated iron.)

Every dish in this chapter is enhanced by an iron pan, which seems to make nearly any food taste more lively. It makes sweet peppers taste sweeter, sears tuna for the best flavor, gives polenta a crisp golden crust, and helps shrimp sizzle. Iron cookware conducts heat in an even, reliable way, perfect for frying. It's also the best choice for high-heat browning and indoor grilling. Before stainless steel and lightweight nonstick cookware came into fashion, iron is what most people used, for good reason. With a little care, these pans last a lifetime—longer, actually.

scorched sweet peppers and onions

Here is a technique you don't hear much about. The idea is to cook peppers and onions in a hot dry pan, relying on the moisture in the vegetables to keep them from burning (though they do char in a pleasant way). Since both the vegetables are high in water content, they begin to steam, but the high heat evaporates the steam immediately. As they are stirred, they start to take on a bit of color and soften. Once they are half-cooked, add salt and a small amount of oil, which allows them to caramelize, intensifying their natural sweetness. Eat them hot or cold. They're good plain, but I usually add garlic, hot pepper, parsley or basil, and a little vinegar too.   SERVES 4

1 large onion, cut into ¼-inch slices

3 medium red or yellow sweet peppers (about 1 pound), sliced into ¼-inch-wide strips

Salt and pepper

2 tablespoons olive oil

2 garlic cloves, minced

Red pepper flakes

1 tablespoon red wine vinegar

Chopped parsley or basil

Heat a wide cast-iron skillet over high heat, without adding any oil or fat, until the pan is nearly smoking, usually 4 to 5 minutes. Throw in the onion and peppers and stir briskly, then continue stirring until the vegetables begin to soften and char slightly, about 2 minutes. Adjust the heat if they seem to be cooking too quickly. Season with salt and pepper, add the olive oil, and stir-fry until nicely caramelized, another minute or so. Add the garlic and a pinch of red pepper flakes and turn off the heat, then transfer to a serving bowl and add the vinegar and chopped parsley or basil.

peppery duck steaks
with parsley salad

This is an easy riff on steak au poivre, made not with beef but with a large, meaty Muscovy duck breast rubbed with a healthy amount of crushed black peppercorns and garlic. The duck is given a beautiful crisp skin in a cast-iron pan and cooked to a rosy medium-rare. Sliced and topped with a simple parsley salad, it makes a generous main course for two or three, or a smaller serving for four.   SERVES 2 TO 4

1 Muscovy duck breast (about 1 pound)

1 teaspoon salt

4 garlic cloves, smashed to a paste with a little salt

1 tablespoon coarsely crushed peppercorns

Parsley Salad (recipe follows)

With a sharp knife, remove the tenderloin from the underside of the duck breast and reserve for another purpose. Trim any ragged bits or gristle. Turn the breast over and trim any excess fat from the edges. Score the skin by making shallow diagonal cuts, ½ inch apart, in one direction and then repeating in the other direction, creating a diamond pattern.

Season on both sides with the salt, then massage with the garlic paste. Press the crushed peppercorns evenly over both sides. Put the duck on a platter and leave to marinate for at least 1 hour at room temperature, or refrigerate overnight (if the latter, bring to room temperature before cooking).

Heat a cast-iron skillet over medium-high heat. After 5 minutes, when the pan is hot, carefully add the duck breast skin side down and let it begin to sizzle. Using tongs, check to see that the skin is not browning too quickly, and reduce the heat as necessary. Be careful, the duck breast will render a fair amount of hot fat. The skin should be golden and crisp after 6 or 7 minutes. Turn the breast over and cook for 2 minutes more. Remove to a carving board and let rest for 10 minutes (when the rendered duck fat has cooled a bit, strain into a jar and save for future use). Cut at an angle into ¼-inch-thick slices and arrange on a platter. Top with the parsley salad and serve.

parsley salad

Parsley can stand up to an assertive, garlicky dressing; indeed, garlic and parsley play very well together.

Think of this salad more as a garnish than a bowlful, as a zippy topping for all kinds of things, from asparagus spears to sliced tomatoes to paper-thin salami. And it's divine too showered over a rosy duck breast or a grilled rib-eye steak, sliced tagliata-style.

1 large bunch flat-leaf parsley

2 teaspoons lemon juice

Salt and pepper

1 small garlic clove, minced

2 tablespoons olive oil

A chunk of Parmigiano-Reggiano
  cheese for shaving (optional)

Pick the parsley leaves from the stems—you want about 2 cups. Wash and gently dry with a clean towel.

In a small bowl, whisk together the lemon juice, salt and pepper to taste, garlic, and olive oil.

The parsley leaves must be dressed at the very last minute. Season with a sprinkle of salt, then toss with the dressing to coat lightly and serve in a fluffy pile. Garnish with shavings of Parmesan, if desired.

griddled polenta scrapple

Scrapple, a traditional Pennsylvania Dutch favorite, is a meaty griddled breakfast dish still featured on menus throughout the mid-Atlantic states. I'm a fan, but I've come up with my own variation that's a little bit Italian (not that any real Italian would ever make it). You start with well-seasoned hot fennel sausage (you can make a small batch for this recipe or buy good-quality Italian sausage), crumbled and lightly fried, and a pot of cooked polenta. Stir them together, and pour into a pie plate to cool. You want to let the whole thing firm up, so do it a day or two in advance. Then cook thick wedges in olive oil until browned and crisp. Good for breakfast, lunch, or supper, and especially nice with a garlicky radicchio salad. SERVES 4

4 cups water

Salt and pepper

1 cup stone-ground polenta

1 pound Pork Sausage (recipe follows) or store-bought spicy Italian fennel sausages

2 teaspoons chopped rosemary

½ cup grated Parmigiano-Reggiano cheese

Olive oil

All-purpose flour for dustng

Bring the water to a boil in a large heavy saucepan. Add 2 teaspoons salt. Whisk in the polenta and stir well. After a minute or two, when the polenta has thickened a bit, reduce the heat to low and let cook gently, stirring occasionally, for about 45 minutes, until the grains have swollen and no raw cornmeal taste remains. (If the polenta gets too dry, add a little more water from time to time.)

Meanwhile, cook the sausage: Heat a wide skillet over medium-high heat. Add the sausage meat (casings removed if purchased) and let it brown,

using a spatula to crumble it into rough pieces, until cooked through, about 5 minutes. Set aside at room temperature while the polenta finishes cooking.

When the polenta is done, add the sausage, along with the rosemary and Parmesan, stirring well to combine. Taste a spoonful of the mixture (let it cool first, so you don't burn your mouth), then adjust the seasoning with salt and pepper. Spread the mixture onto a lightly oiled baking sheet or pie pan (use olive oil) to a depth of ¾ inch. Cool until a skin forms on top, then cover with plastic wrap and let firm up in the refrigerator, preferably overnight.

Heat a large cast-iron griddle or skillet over medium-high heat. Add a thin layer of olive oil. Cut the scrapple into wedges and dust lightly with flour on both sides. Put the wedges "skin" side down on the griddle. Cook gently until nicely browned and crisp, about 4 to 5 minutes, then flip and cook on the other side.

pork sausage

MAKES 1 POUND

1 pound coarsely ground pork
   shoulder, not too lean

1 teaspoon salt

1 teaspoon crushed fennel seeds

½ teaspoon red pepper flakes,
   or more to taste

1 tablespoon sweet paprika

3 garlic cloves, minced

Put the pork in a bowl and add all the remaining ingredients. Mix well to distribute the seasonings evenly. Cover and refrigerate until ready to use, for up to 3 days, or wrap well and freeze for future use.

spanish pork skewers

A delicious hot tapas classic is called *pinchos moruños,* or Moorish skewers—essentially, little kebabs marinated in Arabic (Moorish) spices and grilled, usually on a hot steel plancha. I use a cast-iron pan or griddle. Because Muslim Arabs wouldn't eat pork, one presumes the original dish was made with lamb or goat. Now, however, in most Spanish tapas bars, small cubes of pork are seasoned with garlic, cumin, coriander, pimentón, and sometimes oregano. Once skewered, they need only about five minutes on a hot griddle. Best eaten standing.   SERVES 4

2 teaspoons cumin seeds

2 teaspoons coriander seeds

1½ pounds pork tenderloin, cut into
    ½-inch slices

Salt and pepper

½ teaspoon sweet or hot pimentón

½ teaspoon dried oregano

2 garlic cloves, smashed to a paste with
    a little salt

2 tablespoons olive oil

Lemon wedges

Toast the cumin and coriander seeds in a small dry skillet over medium-high heat just until fragrant, about 1 minute. Finely grind in a spice mill or with a mortar and pestle.

Season the pork lightly on both sides with salt and pepper. Sprinkle with the cumin, coriander, pimentón, and oregano. Mix the garlic paste with the olive oil and drizzle over the meat. Rub the seasonings in with your fingers.

Thread the seasoned pork onto twelve short bamboo skewers. The skewers can be refrigerated for up to several hours.

When ready to cook, heat a large cast-iron griddle or skillet over medium-high heat until nearly smoking. Cook the skewers for about 3 minutes on each side, until nicely browned. Serve hot, with lemon wedges.

sizzling shrimp in the shell

When you cook shrimp this way, the meat stays succulent because it essentially steams within its protective shell as the shrimp fries. The exterior seasoning flavors every bite, and much of the shell is edible, especially the tasty little legs (this is finger food, of course). Fresh wild shrimp in the shell is best, no matter what size. If you use frozen shrimp, choose a sustainable source. SERVES 4

¼ teaspoon Sichuan peppercorns

¼ teaspoon fennel seeds

¼ teaspoon whole cloves

Half a star anise

⅛ teaspoon ground cinnamon

½ cup cornstarch

1½ pounds fresh head-on shrimp or
1 pound medium shrimp in the shell,
rinsed and patted dry

Salt and pepper

½ cup vegetable oil

1 teaspoon finely chopped fresh green
Thai chile or other hot chile

½ cup roughly chopped cilantro

Lime wedges

Grind the Sichuan peppercorns, fennel seeds, cloves, and star anise to a fine powder in a spice mill, and add the cinnamon. Stir this mixture into the cornstarch in a shallow bowl. Dip each shrimp into the seasoned cornstarch, turning to coat, and put them on a plate in one layer. Sprinkle with salt and pepper.

Heat the vegetable oil in a large wok or cast-iron skillet over high heat. When the oil looks wavy, carefully add the shrimp and let them sizzle for about a minute or two on each side, until well crisped. Remove and drain on paper towels.

Transfer the shrimp to a serving dish. Season once more with salt and pepper and sprinkle with the chopped chile and cilantro. Serve with lime wedges, and eat with your fingers.

fragrant sea scallop cakes

Tod mun, a favorite appetizer in Thai restaurants, are little fried fish cakes enhanced with the amazing flavor of kaffir lime leaf. They make a fine snack with drinks, served with a sweet, spicy dipping sauce, or add a pot of jasmine rice and a cucumber salad for a simple meal. Although my version is not completely authentic, it's a fairly faithful homage to the original. Most recipes call for white-fleshed fish, but I like to use sea scallops, which give the cakes a wonderfully light texture. Thai fish cakes are typically deep-fried. These are cooked in a cast-iron skillet in just a little oil, preferably coconut, which adds a sweet and fragrant note.   SERVES 4

FOR THE SCALLOP CAKES

1 pound sea scallops

1/2 teaspoon salt

1/2 teaspoon white or black pepper

2 teaspoons fish sauce

2 small garlic cloves, smashed to a
   paste with a little salt

One 2-inch piece of ginger, peeled and
   grated

6 scallions, thinly sliced

2 teaspoons finely chopped serrano or
   jalapeño chile, or to taste

1/2 cup cilantro leaves and tender
   stems, roughly chopped

2 small kaffir lime leaves, thinly
   slivered

1 small egg, lightly beaten

Coconut or peanut oil for shallow-
   frying

FOR THE DIPPING SAUCE

1/4 cup rice wine vinegar

1/4 cup packed brown sugar

2 or 3 tiny red or green fresh Thai
   chiles, thinly sliced

2 tablespoons chopped or crushed
   unsalted roasted peanuts

2 teaspoons fish sauce

1 teaspoon grated ginger

CONTINUED

To make the scallop cakes, put the scallops in the bowl of a food processor, add the salt, pepper, fish sauce, garlic, and ginger, and process to a fine paste, about 1 minute. Add the scallions, chile, cilantro, kaffir lime leaves, and egg and pulse a few times to combine well. Transfer to a bowl. The scallop mixture can be refrigerated for up to a day.

To make the dipping sauce, combine all the ingredients in a small serving bowl.

Pour coconut oil to a depth of ¼ inch into a wide cast-iron skillet and turn the heat to medium-high. When the oil is hot, carefully add the scallop mixture in large spoonfuls (fry in batches to avoid crowding), adjust the heat if necessary to allow the cakes to brown gently, and cook for about 3 minutes. Flip them, flatten them gently with a spatula, and cook for 2 to 3 minutes more, until browned. Drain on paper towels and serve hot, with the dipping sauce.

bistro chicken liver salad

Composed salads are a staple of old-fashioned French bistro menus, especially at lunchtime. In many, tasty little morsels of some part of a bird are the meaty flourish added to a good green salad—often with those skinny green beans the French love, a crouton or two, and maybe some lardons for good measure. Everything is dressed with a serviceable vinaigrette.

In French, these salads always sound elegant, even if the ingredients are humble, like *salade de gésiers*—made with duck gizzards. *Salade de foie de volaille*—that's chicken livers, bub. But they're always very tasty.

For fun and added flavor, I use the Indian spice blend garam masala. Usually a mixture of cardamom, black pepper, cumin, clove, nutmeg, and cinnamon, garam masala is easy to make at home in a spice mill, or you can buy it ready-made. **SERVES 4 TO 6**

FOR THE VINAIGRETTE

1 tablespoon red wine vinegar

1 teaspoon Dijon mustard

1 garlic clove, smashed to a paste with a little salt

Salt and pepper

3 tablespoons extra virgin olive oil

FOR THE SALAD

½ pound small green beans, topped and tailed

Salt

12 chicken livers (about 1 pound), trimmed

2 tablespoons garam masala, homemade (recipe follows) or store-bought

2 tablespoons clarified butter, ghee, or olive oil

18 cherry tomatoes, halved

6 small handfuls salad greens (5 to 6 ounces)

To make the vinaigrette, mix the vinegar, mustard, and garlic in a small bowl. Add a little salt and pepper, and whisk in the oil.

CONTINUED

To make the salad, cook the green beans in a pot of boiling salted water until barely tender, about 2 minutes. Drain in a colander, cool under cold water, and set aside.

Pat the livers dry with paper towels, then season on both sides with salt and the garam masala. Heat the butter in a wide skillet over medium-high heat. Add the seasoned livers in one layer and let them brown, about 2 minutes. Turn them over and cook for 1 minute more, leaving them pink at the center. Remove from the heat.

Dress the beans and tomatoes with half the vinaigrette, and season with a little salt and pepper. Dress the greens with the rest of the vinaigrette and pile them on a platter or individual plates. Top the greens with the beans, tomatoes, and the warm chicken livers.

garam masala

MAKES ABOUT 2 TABLESPOONS

1 tablespoon cardamom seeds

1 teaspoon black peppercorns

1 teaspoon cumin seeds

1 teaspoon whole cloves

A 2-inch piece cinnamon stick

1/2 teaspoon grated nutmeg

Grind the cardamom seeds, peppercorns, cumin seeds, cloves, and cinnamon in a spice mill. Transfer to a small jar and stir in the nutmeg.

rare-seared tuna
with crushed fennel

The rather aggressive seasonings for this tuna dish mimic those used to make a traditional Italian pork roast: fennel seeds and fronds, black pepper, garlic, and rosemary. They seem completely appropriate for tuna's meaty character. Use the feathery fronds from ordinary fennel bulbs, or wild fennel if it's available. I think this tuna tastes best at room temperature, so I usually cook it a bit ahead. As for accompaniments, a salad of cannellini beans and green beans comes to mind, as does a tomato salad or just a little spicy arugula. Or perhaps all three. SERVES 4 TO 6

1½ pounds yellowfin tuna,
   cut 1½ inches thick

1 teaspoon fennel seeds, crushed

1 tablespoon roughly chopped fennel
   fronds (optional)

½ teaspoon coarsely ground black
   pepper

2 garlic cloves, minced

2 teaspoons roughly chopped
   rosemary

½ teaspoon red pepper flakes

Salt

2 tablespoons olive oil

Put the tuna on a plate. Sprinkle evenly on both sides with the fennel seeds, fennel fronds (if using), black pepper, garlic, rosemary, and red pepper flakes. Season on all sides with salt. Drizzle the olive oil over and then massage in the seasonings. Leave at room temperature for 30 minutes, or refrigerate for up to several hours.

   Heat a wide cast-iron skillet over medium-high heat until nearly smoking. Sear the tuna for about 1 minute on each side, then immediately remove to a serving platter. The fish will continue to cook slightly as it cools, but it should remain rather rare at the center. Cut into thick slices to serve.

crispy potato galette

There is no denying the universal appeal of potatoes cooked until crisp and golden. This is a version of an irresistible old-school French dish called *pommes Anna,* heavenly with a steak, a roast chicken, or just about anything. The key to success is to slice the potatoes very thin and not skimp on the butter. Start the galette in a cast-iron pan on the stovetop and finish it in a hot oven. It serves two civilized people, or one who is gluttonous.   SERVES 2

1 pound russet or large Yellow Finn
    potatoes, peeled

4 tablespoons butter, melted
Salt and pepper

Heat the oven to 400°F, with a rack in the top third. Using a mandoline or sharp knife, slice the potatoes as thin as possible, about $1/16$ inch. Do not rinse or cover with water—the potatoes' starch helps keep the galette intact.

Swirl 2 tablespoons of the butter to coat the bottom of a 10-inch cast-iron skillet. Beginning at the center of the pan, arrange the potato slices in a closely overlapping circular pattern, spiraling outward with each row until the pan is completely covered with slices, all in one layer. Continue until all the slices are used. Season the top with salt and pepper to taste, and drizzle with the remaining 2 tablespoons of melted butter, making sure all the slices are well coated.

Set the pan on a burner over medium-high heat. When the potatoes start to sizzle, let cook for another minute or two, then transfer the pan to the oven. Bake, uncovered, for 20 minutes, or until beautifully browned. To serve, invert the galette onto a cutting board and carefully cut into quarters; alternatively, invert directly onto a serving platter, leaving in one piece.

wok-fried lamb with cumin

The combination of lamb and cumin may conjure up images of Middle Eastern cooking, but lamb and cumin coexist in a number of northern Chinese dishes too—typically paired with lots of hot chile pepper.

During several trips to the vibrant Chinese neighborhood in Flushing, Queens, I found wonderful versions, all equally spicy. In some, lamb breast was braised to utter tenderness and then fried crisp. In others, strips of lamb were stir-fried, as in this recipe. I haven't met a person yet who doesn't love it.

SERVES 3 OR 4

1 pound boneless lean lamb, cut into strips 1/4 inch wide and 1 1/2 inches long

Salt and pepper

1 tablespoon cornstarch

2 tablespoons vegetable oil

1 teaspoon cumin seeds

12 small dried red chile peppers, or more if desired

A 2-inch piece of ginger, peeled and cut into fine julienne

3 garlic cloves, minced

1/2 teaspoon toasted sesame oil

1/2 cup roughly chopped cilantro

6 scallions, thinly slivered

Put the lamb in a small bowl, season with salt and pepper, and sprinkle with the cornstarch. Mix with your fingers to combine.

Heat the vegetable oil in a wok or wide cast-iron skillet over medium-high heat. When the oil is hot, add the cumin seeds and dried chiles. When they begin to sizzle, add the lamb, ginger, and garlic, toss well to coat the lamb, and stir-fry for 1 to 2 minutes, until the lamb is slightly browned. Add the sesame oil, cilantro, and scallions and transfer to a serving dish.

Espresso Hazelnut Bark (page 208)

A LITTLE SOMETHING SWEET

pleasure in small bites

Even if I always claim to never have had much of a sweet tooth, I'll admit to enjoying a few bites of dessert. It doesn't have to be gargantuan; in fact, small desserts always seem more special somehow. Nor must a dessert be rich. Serving some kind of fruit (fresh or dried) and offering a plate of cookies is really all that's necessary for an elegant ending. If it's berries, who could say no to a dollop of whipped cream (just beaten to very soft peaks and not too sweet)? With dessert wine or coffee, another option is to end with something dessert-like, but not a dessert per se, like Espresso-Hazelnut Bark, the Sweet-and-Salty Nut Brittle, or an assortment of diminutive one-bite treats. It's also nice to enjoy something sweet in the afternoon, even making a bit of a ritual of it: I find the little Brown Butter Almond Cakes or the intense, sugary Golden Coconut Cookies are best that way.

espresso-hazelnut bark

I am far from a chocoholic, which puts me in a definite minority at most gatherings. I do, however, appreciate the occasional small nugget, especially if it's on the bitter side. This bark, with its roasty, dark undertones, is a pleasure to pass around the table.   MAKES ABOUT 1 POUND

PHOTOGRAPH ON PAGE 206

3 ounces (about ½ cup) raw hazelnuts

½ ounce (¼ cup) espresso beans

8 ounces bittersweet chocolate, chopped

½ teaspoon flaky sea salt (optional)

Heat the oven to 400°F. Spread the hazelnuts on a baking sheet and roast until well browned and fragrant, 10 to 15 minutes (the skins should look nearly burnt). Put the hazelnuts in a clean kitchen towel and rub briskly to remove the skins. Coarsely chop the nuts. Lightly crush the espresso beans with a rolling pin.

In a double boiler, slowly melt 6 ounces of the chocolate, stirring occasionally until the mixture is smooth. Make sure to keep the heat low, to prevent any moisture or steam from touching the chocolate. When it is completely melted, remove from the heat and stir in the remaining 2 ounces of chocolate. Pour onto a parchment-lined baking sheet, spreading the chocolate to a ¼-inch thickness. Sprinkle the hazelnuts evenly over the surface. Repeat with the crushed espresso beans and the sea salt, if using. Refrigerate, uncovered, until completely hardened.

Break into rough pieces to serve.

after-dinner dates

During the cool months, dates make a nice option for a post-meal sweet. Though simple, they somehow seem luxurious, and I always love eating foods that have been cultivated and treasured for thousands of years. There are many kinds of dates to choose from, but the most commonly available are Deglet Noor, semisweet and firm, and the plump, moist Medjool. In the autumn, you can sometimes get fresh Barhee dates on the branch. Middle Eastern groceries are a good place to buy an assortment of dates and discover which you like best. Adorning a sweet date with a rich filling may seem like gilding the lily, and it is, but you'll be satisfied with only one or two.   SERVES 6

cream-filled dates

½ cup crème fraîche or heavy cream (see Note)

1 tablespoon sugar

½ teaspoon grated orange zest

½ teaspoon grated lemon zest

12 large dates

2 tablespoons coarsely chopped pistachios

Whip the crème fraîche with the sugar in a small bowl until it has the texture of thick yogurt. Stir in the orange and lemon zest.

Split the dates lengthwise with a paring knife and remove the pits. Put a generous spoonful of flavored cream in each hollow. Sprinkle with chopped pistachios.

NOTE: You can substitute mascarpone, ricotta, or even softened goat cheese for the cream.

almond paste dates

½ cup blanched almonds (see Note)

¼ cup granulated sugar

⅛ teaspoon ground cinnamon, plus a
   pinch

1 tablespoon orange flower water

1 tablespoon Demerara sugar or
   coarse raw sugar

12 large dates

Put the almonds, granulated sugar, and ⅛ teaspoon cinnamon in a food processor and grind until the mixture resembles fine cornmeal. Add the orange flower water and pulse to incorporate.

Transfer the mixture to a bowl and knead for a minute, or until it resembles a soft dough; add a few drops of water if necessary. Roll the paste into twelve ½-inch balls, then flatten into almond-shaped ovals. Split the dates lengthwise with a paring knife and remove the pits. Stuff each date with an oval of almond paste and put them on a serving platter.

Mix the Demerara sugar with the pinch of cinnamon in a small bowl. Sprinkle over the dates and serve.

NOTE: To make blanched almonds, drop whole raw natural almonds into boiling water and let steep for 1 minute. Drain, and let cool slightly, then pop the almonds from their skins.

candied grapefruit peel

Candied citrus peel is easy to make at home, and, no slight meant to lemons or oranges, grapefruit peel is my hands-down favorite. Fresh grapefruit juice is a bonus part of this project, which is best completed over several days.

MAKES ABOUT 2 CUPS

6 organic grapefruits

3 cups sugar, plus more for storing
   the peel

2 cups water

Wash and dry the grapefruits. Halve and juice them, reserving the juice for another time, then scrape out the pulp and discard it. Place the rinds in a large stainless steel pot, cover with 6 cups cold water, and bring to a simmer over medium heat. Simmer briskly until firm-tender, about 30 minutes. Drain, then repeat the process with fresh water. Turn off the heat and let the rinds cool in the liquid overnight (this allows them to soften without being overcooked).

The next day, drain and blot dry the rinds. Slice them into strips approximately ¼ inch wide and 2 inches long. Place the strips in a 2-quart stainless steel saucepan, add 2 cups of the sugar and the 2 cups water, and bring to a boil, stirring. Turn down the heat and let simmer until the strips become translucent, about 1 hour. Let cool to room temperature.

Carefully remove the strips (reserve the syrup for another purpose, such as in drinks or as a glaze for baked goods) and spread them out on a metal rack set over a baking sheet. Let dry overnight.

Toss the grapefruit peel with the remaining 1 cup sugar to coat. Store, packed in the sugar, in the refrigerator.

sweet-and-salty nut brittle

This caramelized nut brittle is a bit addictive. Nearly any nut can be a candidate for a one-nut version, but a mixture of nuts, or even seeds, like sesame or pumpkin, makes it more interesting, and a final sprinkling of sea salt adds an especially pleasing note. Break off pieces to serve as after-dinner sweets or with tea or coffee. It can also become a dessert topping, coarsely crushed and crumbled over ice cream. SERVES 6

2 tablespoons butter, softened,
   for the baking sheet
2 cups sugar
1 cup water
½ cup sliced almonds

½ cup pecan halves
½ cup coarsely chopped pistachios
2 tablespoons sesame seeds
½ teaspoon flaky sea salt

Generously butter a 10-by-15-inch baking sheet and set aside. Put the sugar in a 2-quart stainless steel saucepan and slowly add the water, taking care not to splash. Stir just to dissolve the sugar, then bring to a simmer over medium-high heat. Let the liquefied sugar simmer until it begins to take on a little color, about 5 minutes. Continue to simmer, without stirring, until the caramel turns a reddish brown. Remove immediately from the heat (work carefully and quickly, as the caramel will continue to darken from retained heat), and stir in the almonds, pecans, pistachios, and sesame seeds. Pour the mixture onto the prepared baking sheet. Sprinkle with the sea salt and leave the brittle to firm up.

When the brittle is cool, invert to remove it from the pan. Break into pieces and store in an airtight container.

tangerine granita

A good granita that's not too sweet and tastes of real fruit is intensely satisfying. The technique is simple: Fresh fruit juice is sweetened to taste, perhaps with the addition of a few drops of liqueur, then left to freeze, preferably overnight, before it is roughly chopped. There is an ideal moment, in my mind anyway, when the texture of the granita is perfect—not too hard and not too slushy. A glug of Champagne or cava poured over can make it even more impressive. **SERVES 4 TO 6**

½ cup sugar

3 cups tangerine juice
  (from about 3 pounds tangerines)

Juice of 2 large limes

2 tablespoons orange liqueur or kirsch

Champagne or cava (optional)

Put the sugar in a medium bowl and whisk with 1 cup of the tangerine juice until thoroughly dissolved. Stir in the rest of the tangerine juice, the lime juice, and orange liqueur and mix well.

Pour the mixture into a storage container so it comes to a depth of 1 inch and cover it, or pour into a zippered plastic freezer bag and seal well. Freeze for at least 4 hours, or, preferably, overnight.

To serve, chop the frozen mixture roughly with a metal spatula, then spoon into glasses or bowls. Top with a little chilled Champagne if you wish.

golden coconut cookies

The Spanish name of these cookies, *cocadas doradas,* sounds like a very short poem. I first tasted them in a bare-bones family-run bakery in rural Mexico. They had been baked in a homemade *horno* (a clay oven), on hand-hammered cookie sheets made from old license plates. Shredded coconut, piloncillo (a Mexican unrefined sugar), and egg white are the only ingredients. Bake just long enough to crisp and burnish the exterior so the center remains chewy. MAKES 24 COOKIES

2 cups shredded dried unsweetened
   coconut
¾ cup packed light brown sugar or
   piloncillo

½ teaspoon salt
2 large egg whites

Heat the oven to 350°F. Put the coconut in a bowl, cover with boiling water, and steep for 10 minutes. Drain, cool, and squeeze dry.

Put the coconut, sugar, and salt in a food processor and pulse until the coconut is coarsely chopped. Beat the egg whites until just frothy, then add to the mixture. Pulse briefly to combine.

Form the coconut mixture into 1½-inch balls and place on a parchment-lined baking sheet, leaving 1 inch space between them. Pinch each ball to form a slightly pointed top. Bake for 15 minutes, or until golden brown. Leave on the parchment until completely cooled.

ginger spice wafers

These crisp and spicy cookies are perfect for dunking in coffee or wine. Make the dough a day ahead and refrigerate it, so it's firm enough to slice. Or have a batch in the freezer, ready to slice and bake when the mood strikes.

MAKES 36 COOKIES

8 tablespoons (1 stick) butter, softened

¾ cup packed light brown sugar

½ cup granulated sugar

⅓ cup molasses

2 teaspoons grated ginger

1 large egg, plus 1 egg yolk

1 teaspoon brandy

½ teaspoon grated orange zest

2 cups all-purpose flour

1½ teaspoons baking powder

2 teaspoons ground ginger

½ teaspoon ground cinnamon

½ teaspoon finely ground black pepper

¼ cup finely chopped candied ginger, plus more for topping

Put the butter, brown sugar, and granulated sugar in a large bowl. Using a handheld mixer, beat together until creamy. Beat in the molasses, grated ginger, egg, egg yolk, brandy, and orange zest until well combined.

Sift together the flour, baking powder, ground ginger, cinnamon, and black pepper. Slowly add the dry ingredients to the butter mixture, stirring just enough to incorporate. Fold in the candied ginger and chill the mixture until firm.

Put the dough on a floured surface and knead into a long log approximately 2 inches in diameter. Cut the log in half and wrap each half tightly in plastic wrap. Refrigerate for at least several hours, or overnight.

Heat the oven to 375°F. With a sharp thin-bladed knife, cut the dough into ¼-inch slices and place on a parchment-lined baking sheet, leaving ½-inch space in between them. Sprinkle with a little more candied ginger. Bake for about 10 minutes, until lightly browned. Cool on a rack.

brown butter almond cakes

In the style of the French delicacies called *financiers,* these little cakes are made from freshly ground almonds and lightly browned butter, which complements the good almond flavor. They are more appropriately served with tea or coffee than after a meal. The batter is no trouble to whip up, and you can make them any size you like, even bite-sized.

MAKES 12 SMALL OR 24 TINY CAKES

8 tablespoons (1 stick) unsalted butter, plus butter for greasing the molds

½ cup granulated sugar

¼ cup light brown sugar

¾ cup (4 ounces) natural (unblanched) whole almonds

3 large eggs, beaten

1½ teaspoons almond extract

1 tablespoon rum

½ cup all-purpose flour

½ teaspoon salt

½ teaspoon baking powder

Heat the oven to 350°F. Generously butter a standard muffin tin (or 2 mini-muffin tins).

Melt the butter in a small saucepan over medium heat. Let cook until it foams and turns a nut-brown color. Set aside to cool.

Put the two sugars and the almonds in a food processor and grind until the almonds are pulverized, about 1 minute. Transfer to a medium bowl. Add the eggs, almond extract, rum, and browned butter and stir to combine. Sift together the flour, salt, and baking powder. Gradually stir into the almond-egg mixture, then beat to a smooth batter with a whisk or wooden spoon.

For a standard muffin tin, use 2 tablespoons batter per cake (or 1 table-spoon apiece for a mini tin). Rap the tin on a countertop to level the batter and remove any air bubbles.

Bake for 12 minutes (10 minutes for the tiny cakes), until lightly browned. Leave in the tin for 2 minutes, then unmold the cakes and cool them on a rack.

figs with thyme and honey

Although a dried fig may never recapture the juiciness of its ripe state, try this for a winter dessert: start with fat golden Turkish figs, and simmer them in honey and sweet wine, along with thyme and coriander. In the herb-scented syrup, the figs become plump and succulent.

Serve them in small portions—a couple of figs per person is just enough. This method works well with other dried fruits, especially apricots.

SERVES 4 TO 6

12 large dried Turkish figs

2 cups sweet white wine, such as
    Muscat or Tokaji (Tokay)

½ cup mild honey

½ cup sugar

Several fresh thyme sprigs or
    ½ teaspoon dried thyme

1 teaspoon coriander seeds

Juice of ½ lemon

Put the figs in a bowl, cover with boiling water, and let soften for 30 minutes. Drain, then transfer the figs to a stainless steel saucepan. Add the wine, honey, and sugar, and bring to a simmer over medium heat, stirring to dissolve the honey. Add the thyme and coriander and let simmer over low heat for 30 minutes. Turn off the heat and let the figs steep for at least several hours, preferably overnight.

With a slotted spoon, place the figs in a shallow serving bowl. Stir the lemon juice into the remaining syrup (strain the syrup, if desired). Spoon the syrup over the figs. Serve at room temperature.

persimmon and orange salad

It's exciting when piles of bright orange persimmons hit the markets. Squat round Fuyu persimmons are the ones to eat raw, all throughout the fall and winter. No need to wait for them to ripen—eat them firm, peeled, then sliced or wedged. With their sweet musky flavor, they make a lovely salad, combined with other fruits such as oranges and pomegranates, quite refreshing served after a meal.

Note that the larger elongated, pointy Hachiya persimmons must be used fully ripe, so they are unsuitable for this salad. SERVES 4 TO 6

2 large navel oranges or 4 blood
   oranges

2 medium Fuyu persimmons

2 teaspoons sugar

1 teaspoon orange flower water or
   orange liqueur

1 tablespoon chopped pistachios
   (optional)

With a serrated knife, carefully peel the oranges, leaving no white pith. Slice the oranges crosswise into ¼-inch discs.

Using a paring knife, cut around the calyx (top part) of the persimmons with a twisting motion and discard. Peel the persimmons with the knife or a vegetable peeler. Cut each persimmon into 6 or 8 wedges.

Arrange the orange slices on a small platter, then arrange the persimmon wedges on top. Sprinkle evenly with the sugar and orange flower water, and garnish with chopped pistachios, if desired.

VARIATIONS

Fuyu persimmons can be used in savory autumn and winter salads too—with watercress, walnuts, and goat cheese, for instance. Use them as you would pears.

sweet fresh cheese

In classic French bistros, in addition to crème brûlée and tarte Tatin, you can usually get a dessert of *fromage blanc,* a freshly made soft, pure-white cheese. It's brought to the table with a shaker of superfine sugar and maybe a few berries, *fraises des bois* if you're lucky (or it can be eaten with salt and pepper instead, like good cottage cheese). It is a divine little treat. While fromage blanc is widely available in France, that's not the case here. Good ultrafresh ricotta makes a perfect substitute.   SERVES 6

¾ pound (12 ounces) firm fresh
   ricotta (see Note)
½ cup crème fraîche
1 tablespoon milk (if necessary)

Berries (optional)
2 tablespoons superfine or turbinado
   sugar, for sprinkling

Rinse 6 small glasses (shot glasses work well) with cold water. Pack each glass with 2 ounces of the ricotta. Cover with plastic wrap and refrigerate for at least 1 hour.

To serve, invert each glass over a dessert plate. The cheese should unmold easily. Beat the crème fraîche lightly with a spoon to liquefy it, adding a little milk if necessary. Spoon about 1 tablespoon of crème fraîche over each serving.

Garnish each plate with a few berries, if desired. Sprinkle the sugar over the cheese and berries, or pass the sugar at the table.

NOTE: Freshly made ricotta may be purchased at Italian groceries or better cheese stores. Use it immediately, since it turns sour quickly if stored. Shun the commercially produced ricotta sold in most supermarket dairy cases—it usually lacks flavor and has additives as well. If you do find good ricotta or fromage blanc and the texture is too soft to hold a shape when molded, drain it in cheesecloth overnight or serve it in little ramekins instead.

sweet fresh cheese

In classic French bistros, in addition to crème brûlée and tarte Tatin, you can usually get a dessert of *fromage blanc,* a freshly made soft, pure-white cheese. It's brought to the table with a shaker of superfine sugar and maybe a few berries, *fraises des bois* if you're lucky (or it can be eaten with salt and pepper instead, like good cottage cheese). It is a divine little treat. While fromage blanc is widely available in France, that's not the case here. Good ultrafresh ricotta makes a perfect substitute.   SERVES 6

¾ pound (12 ounces) firm fresh
   ricotta (see Note)

½ cup crème fraîche

1 tablespoon milk (if necessary)

Berries (optional)

2 tablespoons superfine or turbinado
   sugar, for sprinkling

Rinse 6 small glasses (shot glasses work well) with cold water. Pack each glass with 2 ounces of the ricotta. Cover with plastic wrap and refrigerate for at least 1 hour.

To serve, invert each glass over a dessert plate. The cheese should unmold easily. Beat the crème fraîche lightly with a spoon to liquefy it, adding a little milk if necessary. Spoon about 1 tablespoon of crème fraîche over each serving.

Garnish each plate with a few berries, if desired. Sprinkle the sugar over the cheese and berries, or pass the sugar at the table.

NOTE: Freshly made ricotta may be purchased at Italian groceries or better cheese stores. Use it immediately, since it turns sour quickly if stored. Shun the commercially produced ricotta sold in most supermarket dairy cases—it usually lacks flavor and has additives as well. If you do find good ricotta or fromage blanc and the texture is too soft to hold a shape when molded, drain it in cheesecloth overnight or serve it in little ramekins instead.

sweet fresh cheese

In classic French bistros, in addition to crème brûlée and tarte Tatin, you can usually get a dessert of *fromage blanc,* a freshly made soft, pure-white cheese. It's brought to the table with a shaker of superfine sugar and maybe a few berries, *fraises des bois* if you're lucky (or it can be eaten with salt and pepper instead, like good cottage cheese). It is a divine little treat. While fromage blanc is widely available in France, that's not the case here. Good ultrafresh ricotta makes a perfect substitute. SERVES 6

¾ pound (12 ounces) firm fresh
   ricotta (see Note)
½ cup crème fraîche
1 tablespoon milk (if necessary)

Berries (optional)
2 tablespoons superfine or turbinado
   sugar, for sprinkling

Rinse 6 small glasses (shot glasses work well) with cold water. Pack each glass with 2 ounces of the ricotta. Cover with plastic wrap and refrigerate for at least 1 hour.

To serve, invert each glass over a dessert plate. The cheese should unmold easily. Beat the crème fraîche lightly with a spoon to liquefy it, adding a little milk if necessary. Spoon about 1 tablespoon of crème fraîche over each serving.

Garnish each plate with a few berries, if desired. Sprinkle the sugar over the cheese and berries, or pass the sugar at the table.

NOTE: Freshly made ricotta may be purchased at Italian groceries or better cheese stores. Use it immediately, since it turns sour quickly if stored. Shun the commercially produced ricotta sold in most supermarket dairy cases—it usually lacks flavor and has additives as well. If you do find good ricotta or fromage blanc and the texture is too soft to hold a shape when molded, drain it in cheesecloth overnight or serve it in little ramekins instead.

Hibiscus Flower Quencher (page 236)

A FEW REMARKABLE DRINKS

an eclectic collection

When the subject of the ideal final meal comes up, in which one gets whatever one wishes for, instead of food I always think about the final drink. But not just a casual "one for the road." I mean, if you could choose one beverage for the last sip you ever take, what would it be? Clear cold water may truly be the best drink of all (not too cold and no ice cubes, please), but stellar options include a frosty beer, a neat whiskey, a well-chilled Negroni, or a perfect espresso. However, the drinks described in this section are not necessarily in that category, even if some might qualify. For the most part, these beverages are meant to satisfy everyday desires.

There are many ways a libation can be of service; it can soothe or nourish, give refreshment, intoxicate, or warm the spirit. What to drink is also a quirky, highly personal choice, dependent upon the hour of day and the season as well as mood or whim. In this chapter I have collected a few favorite drinks, the ones that come to mind most often for me. Some are warm and stimulating, like Real Chai Made to Order, while others are bracing, like the ice-cold Caipiroska. They are distinctly different from each other, yet either could be the right drink at the right time, in a given context.

watered-down wine

It may sound funny to add water to wine, but it actually makes a very nice beverage. And watered-down wine is definitely more food-friendly than sweetened drinks or sodas. Obviously you don't use fine wine to make it, but neither do you use absolute plonk. I prefer to use red wine in about a 50:50 ratio of wine to flat filtered water with the occasional ice cube. (If you use sparkling water, you will have made *tinto de verano,* a traditional Spanish drink, arguably better than any version of sangria.) The ratio of wine to water can vary; sometimes it's only a splash.

It used to be common practice in cafés in France and Italy to order a small carafe of wine and one of water to do the same thing, especially at lunch. Watered-down wine is quite refreshing on a hot day, and it's also a good thing to drink at a cocktail party if you'd rather get home sober.   SERVES 1

3 ounces red wine
3 ounces cold water, preferably
   filtered

Ice cubes (optional)

The method is as follows: Pour the wine into a glass, preferably a tumbler. Add the water and an ice cube or two, if desired.

flavored water for a heat wave

Even though commercially prepared flavored waters abound, I never buy them, since they always taste artificial. The lemon doesn't taste like real lemon, nor does the lime. Just because a label says "natural flavors" doesn't mean it wasn't produced in a laboratory. And even so-called spa water, the sort that you see at saunas and in hotel lobbies, can be too complicated. For sweltering summer days, I prefer to infuse a pitcher of cold water with just a few aromatics. SERVES 4 TO 6

1 small lemon, sliced

1 small cucumber, peeled and sliced

1 small bunch fresh mint

A 2-inch piece of ginger, smashed

7 cups cold filtered water

Ice cubes

Put the lemon, cucumber, mint, and ginger in a 2-quart pitcher. Add the water, then top off the pitcher with ice cubes, and stir. Wait at least 20 minutes before serving, to let the flavors infuse.

hibiscus flower quencher

In Mexico, where hibiscus seems to bloom everywhere, a ruby-red drink called *jamaica* is made from the petals. The dried flowers are steeped like tea in hot water, which is then sweetened to taste. *Jamaica* is pleasantly tannic, which seems to add to its thirst-quenching properties.   SERVES 4 TO 6

PHOTOGRAPH ON PAGE 230

8 cups cold water, preferably filtered

½ cup dried hibiscus petals

½ cup sugar, or to taste

Juice of 1 lime (optional)

Bring the water to a boil in a small stainless steel pot. Add the hibiscus petals and sugar, turn off the heat, and let steep for 15 minutes.

　　Strain the drink and refrigerate until cold. Taste and add the lime juice, if desired. Serve with ice or in chilled glasses.

agua de sandia

Another refreshing Mexican beverage can be made from nearly any ripe fruit and is typically sold ladled from giant glass jars. This one, made from sweet watermelon, is a welcome summer pleasure.   SERVES 4 TO 6

8 cups cubed seeded red or yellow
　　watermelon

Juice of 3 limes, or to taste

½ cup sugar, or to taste

In batches, puree the watermelon in a blender, adding a little cold water if necessary. Pour the watermelon puree into a pitcher, add the lime juice and sugar, and stir. Taste and adjust the sweet-and-sour balance. Thin with more cold water if you wish, and refrigerate.

Aqua de Sandia

a cultured drink

In hot climates, when dairy drinks are consumed, they tend to be the cultured kind, like yogurt, buttermilk, or kefir. A delicious example is this Indian-style lassi, a yogurt drink that can be sweet or lightly salted. Here is an easy salted version.　SERVES 1

½ teaspoon cumin seeds

1 cup plain yogurt

1 teaspoon grated ginger

Good pinch of salt

Small pinch of cayenne

Juice of ½ lime

6 large ice cubes

Toast the cumin seeds in a small dry pan until fragrant, about 1 minute. Coarsely grind in a spice mill or with a mortar and pestle.

In a small bowl, whisk together the yogurt, ginger, cumin, salt, cayenne, and lime juice. Add the ice cubes and let the mixture chill for 5 minutes, then strain into a tall glass.

VARIATION

An even simpler summer beverage is cold buttermilk, poured over ice cubes and seasoned with salt and pepper.

provençal cocktail

Summer is the time to enjoy Pastis, the potent anise-tinged beverage that's a favorite around the Mediterranean. Most people drink it diluted with ice water; it goes down easily in sweltering weather. I like it just fine, but for a refreshing aperitif with a bit of spritz, I make a Pastis-flavored syrup and add it to a glass of sparkling Prosecco or cava.

FOR THE PASTIS SYRUP

1 cup sugar

1 tablespoon crushed fennel or
   anise seeds

1 small lemon, sliced

2 cups water

½ cup Pastis

Chilled Prosecco or cava

To make the syrup, put the sugar, fennel seeds, lemon, and water in a small stainless steel saucepan and bring the mixture to a boil. Reduce the heat to low and simmer for 10 minutes. Turn off the heat and let cool. Add the Pastis.

Strain the syrup and store in a bottle in the refrigerator.

To serve, put 1 tablespoon syrup in a wineglass and slowly pour in chilled Prosecco or cava.

caipiroska

The well-known Brazilian caipirinha is made with cachaça, a liquor distilled from sugarcane. Equally popular throughout South America is the caipiroska, a vodka-based drink made in a similar way with lots of fresh lime. The limes are pounded with sugar first, before the ice and vodka are added. Caipiroskas are best served with a beach in view, on the beach itself, or with a beach in mind. **SERVES 1**

2 small limes, quartered

1 tablespoon sugar

2 ounces vodka

Ice cubes

Put the limes and sugar in a cocktail shaker or sturdy glass. Mash vigorously with a wooden muddler or pestle. Add the vodka and a few ice cubes, shake well, and pour into a rocks glass.

gunpowder
and fresh mint tea

The communal aspect of sharing a pot of tea is a ritual I admire. In Morocco, fragrant mint tea is synonymous with hospitality, offered before and after meals and anytime in between. The water is always freshly boiled and it is customary to prepare the tea in full view of one's guests. It's a simple business: into the pot goes a large bunch of fresh mint and a small amount of the green tea called gunpowder. Traditionally it's served quite sweet in small decorative glasses. I prefer it lightly sweetened, or sometimes not sweet at all. SERVES 6

4 cups water

1 large bunch mint

2 teaspoons gunpowder
  green tea leaves

6 lumps raw sugar

Bring the water to a boil in a teakettle. Pour a bit of the boiling water into a 3-cup teapot to warm it, then discard. Put the mint, tea, and sugar in the teapot and pour the rest of the boiling water over. Let steep for 3 to 5 minutes.

Pour into small glasses to serve.

lemongrass tisane

Typically a tisane is a noncaffeinated tea made by steeping flavorful herbs or flowers in hot water. A sturdy herb like lemongrass needs a little simmering to coax out more flavor. Wild claims have been made for its health benefits, but I make lemongrass tisane just because I love the flavor.   SERVES 4

A 6-inch length of lemongrass, tender center only, thinly sliced

4 cups water

Put the lemongrass in a stainless steel saucepan, add the water, and bring to a boil. Reduce to a bare simmer and cook for 2 minutes, then let steep for 5 minutes. Strain into a warmed teapot and pour into small cups.

hot ginger tea

Boil a handful of peeled, sliced fresh ginger in a saucepan of water for a few minutes, then add a little honey or sugar. It is a soothing but stimulating drink. Ginger tea can also be a home remedy for cold or flu, in which case a little sliced garlic and some cayenne should be added to the pan.   SERVES 4

4 cups water
A 3-inch piece of ginger, peeled and thinly sliced

2 tablespoons honey, or to taste
6 thin lemon slices (optional)

Bring the water to a boil in a small saucepan. Add the ginger, reduce the heat, and simmer gently for 10 minutes. Stir in the honey to dissolve.

Strain the tea into warmed cups. Add a lemon slice to each, if desired.

Lemongrass Tisane

real chai made to order

A friend who had spent a lot of time in India made "real" chai from scratch for me many years ago. This was long before America went chai crazy, applying the name to a bewildering range of drinks. In the traditional preparation, fragrant toasted spices are pounded by hand, then steeped with hot milk and black tea. The extraordinary flavor is well worth the small effort of making it at home. SERVES 2

½ teaspoon fennel or anise seeds

4 green cardamom pods

6 whole cloves

A 1-inch piece of cinnamon stick

½ teaspoon black peppercorns

1 bay leaf

A 1-inch piece of ginger, peeled and
    thinly sliced

2 cups milk

1 tablespoon black tea leaves,
    preferably Assam or Ceylon

Raw sugar or brown sugar

Lightly toast the fennel seeds, cardamom, cloves, cinnamon, peppercorns, and bay leaf in a small dry pan over medium-high heat just until fragrant, about 1 minute.

Crush the spices a bit in a spice mill or with a mortar and pestle, then transfer to a stainless steel saucepan. Add the ginger and pour in the milk. Bring to a gentle simmer and cook for 2 minutes. Add the tea leaves, turn off the heat, cover the pot, and let steep for at least 5 minutes.

Strain the chai into warmed cups and sweeten to taste.

afterword

I am happy to share this little collection with you, and hope that perhaps in some way the book has inspired you to explore some of your own favorite dishes as well.

I also hope you don't follow the recipes slavishly, since improvisation and ad-libbing are always part of a good cook's process—they make life in the kitchen much more interesting. Feel free to personalize these dishes, and use them as templates for versions that express your own idea of pleasure.

One word of counsel, though. A few ingredients and a sure hand can produce wonderful results. Most cooks tend to overcomplicate. Restraint can be admirable. Often, a dish needs less instead of more; sometimes just a squeeze of lime at the last minute is the perfect solution.

acknowledgments

Merci mille fois to the team at Artisan for their unwavering friendship, support, and expertise: Ann Bramson, Trent Duffy, Judith Sutton, Nancy Murray, Michelle Ishay-Cohen, Kara Strubel, Bridget Heiking, Allison McGeehon, and Lia Ronnen.

As always, a huge thanks to Katherine Cowles.

I especially thank Dorothy Kalins, Joan Simon, and Betsy Klein for their invaluable assistance. My sincere gratitude goes to Andrea Gentl and Marty Hyers.

Grazie mille to Randal Breski, Barbara Tanis, Fabrizia Lanza, Ignacio Mattos, Carl Paganelli, Charles Kaiser, Russell Moore, the Gilberts, the Gordons, Bob Cannard, Tony Oltranti, Robert Carrau Jr., Alice Waters, Emily Weinstein, the Chino family, Amy Dencler, Maggie Trakas, B&S, and Davia Nelson.

Thanks a million to Emma Lipp, Jeremiah Stone, Stephanie Sugawara, Alexandra Schmidt, Megan McDiarmid, and Emma Cline for recipe testing, countless sundry tasks, and for their good cheer.

index